Rabbiting Man

By

Fred J Taylor

FRED J TAYLOR

Rabbiting Man

Illustrations by
TED ANDREWS

COCH-Y-BONDDU BOOKS
2007

First published in 2007 by Coch-y-Bonddu Books

ISBN No. 1-904784-11-9

ISBN No. 978-1-904784-11-1

Published and distributed by
Coch-y-Bonddu Books
Machynlleth, Powys, SY0 8DJ
Tel: 01654 702837   www.anglebooks.com

INTRODUCTION

Rabbits and I go back a long, long way. So far back that I do not remember a time when they were not part of my life. From my earliest childhood rabbit was frequently served at the table, along with many other types of game and wild food. I started rabbiting when I was still at school. Then later, when there was rationing after the war and we were glad to get any meat that we could put on the table, I fed my family on rabbits and other wild game. I have so many happy memories of the eighty years since I caught my first rabbit that I cannot begin to put them into chronological order. I have just pieced together a few of my fond recollections of rabbiting and my life in the countryside.

It would be impossible for me to list all of the many friends that I have made in a lifetime of rabbiting. However, one man stands out from the rest. His name was Ralph Rayner and he taught me all that I know of rabbiting, and a good deal more besides. I was privileged to have been taught by him, and to have learned so much from his skill in the field.

I have written before about many of my rabbiting exploits. I would like to thank the Editor of Shooting Times Magazine, for whom

I have written over nearly 40 years for allowing me to use extracts from my previously written work. I would also like to thank Malcolm Baldwin and Alec Martin who have been my constant companions. Although they are very much younger than I am, they have tolerated my old age and infirmity over the years with sincerity. I appreciate their kindness and their help and I wish them well.

I must also thank my special Aussie sporting friends, the late Ernie Chitty, Ron Hoffner, Laurie Hately, Bert Geddes and Phil Green. We had wonderful times together.

I have ended each chapter with a rabbit recipe or two. These have been published before but I welcome this opportunity to offer them to a new generation of rabbiting folk.

CHAPTER 1

I find it hard to believe that it is about eighty years since I shot my first rabbit. In the long summers of my childhood my pals and I used to camp out for weeks on end. Our favourite site was close to a big hillside warren which held lots and lots of rabbits. We had a little 8mm garden gun, which took a half-penny cartridge and was just about capable of killing the smaller rabbits. It certainly couldn't handle the big ones, which were too crafty for us anyway. We would sit quietly near the warren until the young rabbits came out and started to play. If we were lucky we would shoot two or three before taking them back to camp and frying them over our camp-fire. Our supplies consisted of a pound of lard and half a sack of potatoes, and our kit was limited to several frying pans and black billy-cans. Despite our meagre rations and paucity of equipment we enjoyed ourselves enormously. We were very lucky that our parents allowed us such freedom.

I have caught rabbits by all manner of methods. I have even caught many with my bare hands, especially in Australia. However I have caught more rabbits by ferreting than by any other method. Ferreting is not a fly-by-night venture. It has to revolve around a complete season's care and attention. The ferrets have to be bred and reared, and, although they hunt naturally without training, they do have to learn to come to hand. So becoming a ferreter really starts with the breeding of the young ferrets. These can be handled at a very early stage and the love and devotion of the mother ferret is obvious and is transferred, I feel sure, to the human being who looks after them.

There are many things to consider when rearing and breeding ferrets but one of the main problems has to do with the large numbers of young kits which are bred every year. The female ferret comes into season and must be mated. If she is not allowed to mate at this time she may become debilitated and can even die. Thus there are always more young bred than are really required. The trouble with having too many kits used to be that they were sold at ridiculously cheap prices at country shows and markets. The breeders were prepared to accept as little as half-a-crown each for these unwanted kits and they were often sold well before they should have left their mother.

When we formed a Ferret Society many, many years ago, someone mentioned the fact that we ought really to give the hob, or male, ferret a vasectomy. This, he said, would allow the mating process to take place but no kits would follow. Although I don't know whether he was joking or not, I thought seriously about having a male ferret vasectomised. I put the idea to a local vet who said, "I have no idea how to do the job but I will figure it out". I took along two hobs and I asked him to operate on both of them. He performed the operation very successfully indeed and I am quite sure that I was the first one to have this done. It cost me £18 for each ferret to have the operation but I reckoned it was well worth it. These days vasectomised hobs are available all over the country and it is now normal procedure to let the couples mate but not to produce too many kits. It has been a great success and I do take a certain credit for introducing this idea. My veterinary surgeon is also to be congratulated.

Years ago it was the custom to muzzle or cope the working ferret. The ferrets were generally starved before they were worked so that they went down into the bury to work and chase rabbits out in a keen and hungry state. If they did catch one and they were not muzzled they would proceed to eat it. Today the muzzle is practically unheard of. They are still available but they are generally regarded as wicked pieces of equipment especially the metal cope. In the old days the ferreting man used to muzzle them with a piece of string, which was quite an art in itself.

We also have electric collars and above-ground receivers so that we know roughly which routes the collared ferrets running loose underground are taking. All this has to be taken into consideration and although it does not take a genius to learn how to do it, it does have to be learned. It is not simply a question of putting a ferret down a hole and letting it do the rest. There is far more to it than that, as anyone who tackles the job will find out in due course.
All these things had to be learned over the years. Today we once again have thousands of rabbits and a new generation of ferreters are practicing successfully and humanely.

Wiring or snaring can be a very effective way of controlling rabbits. As, also, was the use of the old-fashioned gin-trap, now thankfully barred. We still have the humane trap, however, which catches the rabbit around the neck and kills it immediately. It is more humane but from the point of view of producing carcasses, less efficient. All these things have to be considered but I still believe that ferreting is the most enjoyable form of catching rabbits and of producing good carcasses at the end of the day.

There are plenty of good books dedicated to the technical procedures of ferreting. I am not attempting to teach anything technical here, but to convey a feeling of the enjoyment and the fine sport to be had in a day's ferreting, and of the satisfaction to be gained from taking home fine, wholesome food for the table.

FRIED RABBIT

Young rabbits may be split down the middle, dusted with seasoned flour and fried with bacon rashers or streaky pork slices. This is, in my opinion, one of the most delicious of all game dishes. Very young rabbits can be dipped in an egg or flour-and-water batter, rolled in bread-crumbs and deep fried.

CHAPTER 2

You could say, I suppose, that I come from a rabbiting family. My father and uncles were keen on ferrets, traps, snares, long-nets and any method of catching rabbits without, I have to say, being too particular about where they went! They were not strictly poachers. They had permission to ferret here and there but very often they strayed over boundary hedges when they were not really entitled to do so. They also followed the local hunt as a means of discovering new buries in territory which they could not normally cross, in the hopes of setting a long-net later under cover of darkness. This somewhat unconventional method accounted for many of their rabbits. My uncle swore, too, that there was a time when he was apprehended for "loitering with intent to kill a coney"!

Rabbits were treasured when they were thick upon the ground and, although farmers complained bitterly about having too many, they were very, very cautious about letting ferreters or rabbiters of any description go in search of them. It is said that many of the farm rentals were paid purely and simply out of rabbit carcasses, and I certainly believe this was the case.

I was taught how to set snares at a very early age and I was shown how to put my fist through the noose and extend the fingers of my right hand fully to get the correct distance from the ground. I used an ordinary pricker made from a twig cut from the hedgerow, but today I use bent wire prickers which don't turn in the wind, hold the noose in exactly the correct position and are very much easier to handle.

I was also taught how to set gin-traps, but I was never was very happy using them. There can be no question but that they were an effective means of catching rabbits, whether set in the open or in a warren. In those days I used a small trowel to hack out enough of the ground cover to hide the trap and set it "tittle" so that any rabbit treading on the trap would be caught. It always did seem cruel to me but, again, I cannot deny it was efficient.

Today I use the humane trap and I have a bundle of aluminium sticks which I had made from off-cuts when I was working for a fishing tackle company. These would have been wasted so I made a 100 or so walking-stick pegs for use with the traps. I later learned to use them on very hard ground with purse-nets when ferreting and they were particularly useful in Australia where the ground is hard and rocky.

It is said that neglect of traps, up to a certain point, is advisable and a certain amount of rust goes unnoticed, or is taken little heed of, by rabbits, but of course this neglect must never be allowed to affect the action of the trap. I use a small paint brush to grease the hinges every so often and then I chuck them on to an old dung heap, which imparts an outdoor natural smell and I find this is ideal. My traps are never shiny and they are well camouflaged.

Nowadays I scoop out the necessary layer of dirt from the entrance to the bury by using a trap hammer. I wouldn't know where to buy one in Britain for I brought mine back from Australia many years ago and it has proved invaluable. On one end of the stick is a hammer for driving home the heavy iron or aluminium peg holding the trap and on the other end is a hoe arrangement which literally scrapes out all the dirt necessary without any undue effort. It is an ideal tool and I would hate to be without it.

I don't know how much longer I shall be privileged to go out all night with traps and snares but it gets harder on each occasion because there seem to be fewer rabbits about. In the old days twenty rabbits would have been considered to be a reasonable reward for a night's snaring or trapping, but on my last two outings both traps and snares resulted in seven rabbits on each occasion. Seven rabbits are hardly worth spending a night in the country for, though it is still, to me, an adventure. If one can cook a meal on a campfire and remain comfortably warm, it is a pleasure regularly to visit the snares and traps to make sure that a caught rabbit does not remain there too long.

I am well aware that some people set their traps and snares and leave them all night and while I agree that it is unwise to visit them too often, I feel humanity should prevail and a freshly caught rabbit in a snare should be quickly removed and despatched. The humane trap rarely catches a rabbit by the foot but just occasionally things go wrong and a rabbit is foul-caught and has to be killed quickly. All my rabbiting has been as humane as possible. That is the way I was taught, and the way I shall always continue.

RABBIT PARCELS

Remove the bones of a rabbit's rear leg and cut into, as near as possible, two equal portions. Lay out on the table 4 thin slices of streaky bacon, one travelling east and west, and the other three on top of it travelling north and south. On top of this place the half rabbit leg. On top of that place some stuffing of your liking, sage and onion preferably. On top of that place the second portion of rabbit and then simply flip over the bacon portions to cover everything up. Do not squeeze tightly and pack several of these into a small dish before baking them off with a knob of butter and pepper (but no salt). Allow one parcel per person.

CHAPTER 3

There have been places where it has been vital for me to make a grand show of rabbit clearance. One such farm, only a mile-and-a-half from where I live, and not much more than 100 acres, was over-run to the extent that rabbits were playing on the drive in the front of the house. We were asked, there and then, to deal with the situation to the best of our ability, but it took more than one outing to bring the situation under control.

In fact, the farm was near one of our fishing waters and we liked to go there for the carp which ran, if you were lucky, to maybe seven pounds. It was generally accepted that people didn't fish at night, but there was nothing in the club rules to that effect so Malcolm and I would run our long-net and spend our nights fishing for carp at one and the same time. It was to be two seasons hard work before we made any real impression on the rabbits and even when we had reduced numbers to a minimum, the farmer assured us that he had still got plenty left. Of course, he hadn't but farmers are farmers!

It was not a particularly easy rabbiting situation because many of the banks were steep and one warren, in the very middle of a field, was huge and very deep. We had to do our best with four ferrets and a liner, as well as a long-net, lamping at night, traps, snares and any other method we could think of. We would start fishing at dusk, wait until about midnight and then run out the long-net. This was very successful on one occasion during the summer months and we caught eight pregnant does, kept them alive, and took them over to another farm where the farmer had expressed a wish to see a few rabbits running about, for there were none there. We took the does over in the early hours of the morning, poked them down an old warren and had very fine rabbiting there for many years!

One of the most maddening things that can happen when running a long-net at night is to catch a hedgehog! There is only one way out of it, as far as I am concerned, and that is to cut the net around the creature and repair it later. I cannot think of any other way of getting a rolled-up hedgehog out of a long-net, especially in the darkness.

At that farm we took over 100 rabbits in one small field and didn't shoot one of them. We once caught, I recall, 31 rabbits in snares at night and I also took one or two in the long-net by using the lamp and making them run towards the net.

There were some very steep banks which we were obliged to stink out to move the rabbits into nearer and smaller buries. This worked very, very successfully. I have since learned how to soak potatoes or crab apples with oil and creosote and then to roll them into the holes but, on that occasion I simply tore up sheets of old newspaper, took a bucketful of creosote and blocked up all the holes except two or three, so allowing the rabbits to escape and take up residence in nearby buries. It is a very good method because it moves the rabbits from the more difficult situations into easier ones which are workable with ferrets. It also causes the rabbits to become overcrowded and consequently to bolt easier.

The farm itself was situated on the site of a former brick-pit. There was an old kiln there but many of the hedgerows were raised well above the ground which had been excavated, and the result was that the rabbits could bury very deeply and were difficult to get at with ferrets. They certainly could not be dug.

We also used the ferrets in another high-bank situation and bolted a few into the net but, at long last, were obliged to admit that we had lost a jill ferret. At that time we did not have electronic collars and receivers but, quite frankly, I don't believe they would have helped in the least. We enlarged the surface holes so that we could grope around with withy and bramble sticks to see if we could locate the jill but, in the end, we found some old roofing slates, covered the holes with these and with dirt, and left a supply of food and straw for the ferret should it decide to come back.

Malcolm and I, with only a couple of miles to travel, went daily to look for our lost ferret, but to no avail and it was several weeks before she turned up. By good fortune Malcolm was there when the little jill came to the surface. There was no problem with picking her up, even though she had been living totally wild, obviously killing rabbits and other small animals to survive. She had very little hair left on her body but was surprisingly placid and willing to be picked up. In fact, I think she was happy to be back in human care again. We treated her with special attention as she had returned to us and, in due course, she bred us a litter of ferrets which stood us in good stead and continued the line we had struggled very hard to maintain.

There is a lot more to ferreting than just catching rabbits. The care of ferrets is a year-round task as one is obliged to look after stock and to continue the breeding process to produce healthy, happy and quiet ferrets.

BAKED RABBIT I

Soak in salt water over-night. Drain, dredge with flour, and brown in oil or fat in a hot pan. Place in baking pan. Make gravy with grease in which rabbit has browned. Pour gravy over browned rabbit. Bake at 350° until tender - about one hour.

BAKED RABBIT II

One large rabbit cut in serving pieces. Dredge in seasoned flour and brown in hot fat or bacon drippings in a heavy skillet. Place in a roasting pan and pour the drippings over the rabbit. Add a cup of water, a tablespoon of Worcestershire sauce and a dash of Tabasco. Bake at 350° for one-and-a-half hours or until tender. More liquid may have to be added as the rabbit cooks.

CHAPTER 5

In a long lifetime spent among rabbit buries, in woods, around water-sides and in the open air, practising one form of field sport or another, I have never been in serious trouble in England. It is true that I have fallen into many waters at different times and I have come home wet through, covered in mud, and feeling very sorry for myself, but I have never been in what I consider to be grave danger. Nor have I had any fears. I do not like being out alone in the dark without a companion although I am not, strictly speaking, afraid of being alone in the dark. It is just that I am conscious that if anything goes wrong then I have no help to hand and I believe it is always wise to take a companion on a night venture.

There was one occasion in Australia, however, when I was worried and was in danger. Bill, Phil and I had permission to go rabbiting in the outback about ten miles from the nearest road, some distance from our homes. Bill had a beat-up old pick-up truck which he used specifically for such outings as ferreting and night-spotting rabbits. We had three days at our disposal and we were going to make the most of it. Ice was packed in the cooler boxes and nets were laid out so that they could be pressed firmly home with walking-stick shaped pegs of metal rather than wood. The Australian outback is often very hard and nets with metal pegs tend to tangle up so we kept nets and pegs separately.

We had an enjoyable first day, and caught about eight rabbits. This was nothing very special so while the two other fellows went out with the spot-lamp to try and pick off a few more, I made camp. We had pitched a big tent for three of us and I lit the campfire, made a wind-break and skinned a couple of young rabbits ready for eating. Now it's rather strange that in Australia you can cook rabbits while they are still warm, and they will still be tender at the end of the operation. I've never tried it in England and it has gone against the grain, but I've done it many times in Australia. I do know that there you can go out, kill a rabbit, and cook it within minutes to sheer perfection. Perhaps there is just a little difference in the liquid content of the rabbits in the Australian outback!

However, having achieved the first day's catch, skinned and put them on ice, we went to bed and arose early to give the ferrets a run on a completely new area. That was when the trouble started.

As the sun rose higher, the sand seemed to get deeper and less negotiable and in the end the old pick-up truck decided it had had enough, conked out and would not restart. This was no joke. We were ten miles from the nearest road and walking back to civilisation would have been very, very unpleasant if not dangerous. We had food and we had water but the chances of anyone coming out to see if we were in trouble were precisely nil. "This," I said, "is not funny", and Bill bit his lip, threw his hat on the ground and said "Who the hell said I thought it was?" I could see that he was not only angry but he was also pretty scared too.

Phil kept very calm throughout the whole episode and eventually we got our heads together and decided that we would try and move the truck. As it happened, it was on a fairly level, hard piece of ground but it still took a lot of effort to inch the truck forward slowly as the three of us pushed it. We cleared a track behind it as we moved forward and when we considered we had enough room, Bill sat in the driver's seat and Phil and I pushed it backwards. The truck rolled back and, as it gathered just a little speed, Bill released the clutch and, thank goodness, the vehicle started. Once started it kept going and we were in no serious trouble after that. What we did then was to visit the various warrens but keep the truck's engine running. Then, leaving the ferrets and nets at the warren, we would drive to the nearest hill and leave the truck at the top so that we could bump-start it by rolling it downhill.

We laughed about it as we progressed, and afterwards too, but in reality it was not a funny situation in the outback of Australia in such tremendous heat. Remember, rabbits are hunted there in the heat of the summer when they are not breeding because of the lack of moisture. The extreme heat in the outback and bush-land is crippling, and it is essential to take a drink every 20 minutes or so. It is a marvellous and most enjoyable situation when things are going well but when they are not it can be very worrying! The Australian outback is not the place to be stranded in at any time!

During that three-day adventure we harvested, I suppose, about 28 rabbits. Nothing to write home about but a most enjoyable experience and again, as is the case with most of the rabbits I have ferreted in Australia, they were all free-bolters. During the daytime, moving from warren to warren, we kept the gutted carcasses in a wet sack, hung over the 'roo bars in front of the old truck. Then, when nightfall came and we retired to camp, each took our turn at skinning, dressing out, chopping up our rabbits and placing them on the ice. Containers holding a couple of gallons of frozen water lasted a lot longer than the free ice with which we loaded the other containers. It is always a good idea to put bottles of water into the ice containers because it lasts so much longer. It also ensures a further supply of drinking water in a harsh environment.

Australian ferreting is very different to that in Britain and one has to remember to keep the ferrets in the open air as much as possible, so we carried them in cages rather than warm boxes. We laid a wet sack on top of the cage and put it in the shade so that the ferrets were kept cool. This is very unlike our situation at home when we try to keep the ferrets out of the wind and in a warm situation.

There are vastly more rabbits to be harvested in Australia than in England (or there were at the time I am speaking about) but it is a different situation entirely. It is a question of adjusting from being able to walk along crunchy ice-filled puddles at home to tolerating the hot Aussie sun. The temperature can be up to and above 100°F but there again rabbiting is rabbiting. I guess it doesn't matter too much which part of the world you are in while you're doing it.

RABBIT PATTIES

Cut raw or cooked rabbit into rather small dice and mix with a lesser amount of diced bacon, season liberally with salt and pepper, mix well, and moisten with stock or water. Have ready some patty-tins lined with short-crust or puff pastry, fill them with the meat mixture, and put on the pastry covers. Brush over with egg and bake in a moderately hot oven for about 20 minutes, or until cooked if using raw meat. Serve either hot or cold.

CHAPTER 6

Malcolm and I started rabbiting early in the season some years ago and probably should have known better. There had been no signs of young rabbits around for weeks, however, and the time seemed ripe enough. A fairly long, dry spell at the end of summer had helped discourage breeding, we thought, for we both believe that moisture is essential to breeding, and so we put the young ferret stock to work at the end of September.

For weeks a local farmer had told of large numbers of big rabbits running freely over two meadows, and signs of well-used buries along all the hedgerows had borne out his observations. Nettles were high, green and vicious when we started work, but we're used to being stung half to death in the early weeks, and anyway we were as keen to get started as the farmer was to see the end of the infestation. It was to be one of our disappointing days, however. One fine rabbit bolted within seconds, but the next few sets produced tiny rabbits that came from all directions. Malcolm and I picked up the nets and made for home, deciding, very quickly, to leave that particular area for another month. Old Jill, the labrador, who didn't really care for ferreting because she had to sit and watch, but who nevertheless insisted always on coming, was allowed to hunt the thick cover on the way back to the truck. As if to say "I can do it as well as those things in the bag" she turned out and neatly caught an adult rabbit with only a few yards to go. She presented it to Malcolm with much tail-thumping pleasure, and we duly went home with a dinner apiece. Honour was saved, but only just.

A dozen or so miles away, we had earlier cleared several buries of their tall nettles in advance, knowing full well that rabbits might vacate as a result. They did, of course. We spent best part of the next morning listening to one rabbit being chased round an underground cavern and ended up with another pair, one of which came as the result of a dig. The hold-up was a long way from the entry holes and, despite my past bad experiences with electronic collars and receivers; I know that some ferret locators are extremely accurate and do all that is claimed of them. I would not complain if I never had need of a locator again, but the accuracy of the one we used that day, regarding both location and depth, gave me a feeling of comfort.

On that same farm, a week later, after we considered that the effects of the mass clearing operation had died down, we worked the young jills again in a steep bank set. They hunted naturally and with great enthusiasm but, as is always the case with youngsters, they had no experience of purse-nets. Their frantic hunting displaced net after net, and the occasional tangling they encountered made them excited. This is a critical time for young jills. It is frustrating having to re-set nets continually and, after having used experienced older jills that come immediately to hand when called, the reluctance of excited youngsters can be annoying. These first few outings, however, constitute their initiation to their task, and decide what kind of workers they will turn out to be, and a great deal of patience is required at this stage. They may refuse to come to hand and, in their excitement, start to nip. It is not intentional on their part but snatching, grabbing and squeezing them now may make them temperamental in the future. It is vital to let them come in their own good time and to allow them to sniff the outstretched hand for reassurance. Talking when rabbiting does not help at all, but it is essential, occasionally, to murmur quietly to inexperienced ferrets.

Two of ours undoubtedly learned to kill during that one hunt. Having done so, they were keen to carry on and, in the process, located and bolted five young rabbits that slipped through the meshes and escaped. Our tally that day comprised three good rabbits, one of which was "set" with young, but not in milk. These results, by our usual standards, were decidedly poor, but we had not yet viewed our best territory, so we ventured further afield to a big warren on the banks of a large gravel-pit. The ground was soft and sandy, and the signs of rabbit were all that the owners had claimed. We put down seventy nets in all; confident that this was to be our first bonanza of the season, but again there was disappointment. After a strangely long period of inactivity, during which time all the jills showed at the surface several times, we accounted for six rabbits, four of which were stricken with myxomatosis! It was a sad state of affairs. A few weeks previously the grass had been trimmed short by a host of healthy rabbits; today there was nothing to encourage another hunt and we left well alone!

However, seven miles to the west was another deep complex and we decided to try an early session there. As well we did. Although deep, the bury seemed only to be occupied in the top layer and, although a small number of rabbits in a vast area were able to dodge our three ferrets for a time, we finally had them backed up in two dead ends. Using a lined hob we located two bunches of five and all were harvested. Admittedly some digging was required but it was worth it.

All of which goes to show that all of ferreting is not sheer skill. Who knows what the result would have been had our quarry gone into the deeper tunnels? Would they have bolted cleanly from the deeper sets? Would we have ended up with a nightmare digging scenario in a six feet deep complex? Would we have ended up with a few mangled corpses because of the depth involved? But then I guess that is half the fun of rabbiting in general, although I know full well that it doesn't pay to start too early!

SOUTHERN BAKED RABBIT I

Skin, clean and joint two young rabbits, and soak overnight in cold water to which has been added a little vinegar. When ready to cook, drain and dry well. Rub with salt, pepper and butter, place in a heavy baking pan, and put in a 400°-oven for 15 minutes. Meanwhile, chop two onions finely and put in an iron skillet with four tablespoons of melted butter. Brown lightly, add a little flour and brown well. Add some chopped mushrooms, diced ham, a clove of garlic, parsley and thyme, a bay leaf, and about two cups boiling water. Cook, stirring until smooth. Pour over the rabbits, return to the oven, bake slowly for 20 minutes, basting frequently. Serve with cornbread.

SOUTHERN BAKED RABBIT II

Skin, clean and joint two young rabbits, and soak overnight in cold water to which has been added a little vinegar. When ready to cook, drain well, flour and brown in butter with two chopped onions, salt and pepper. Add one can of mushroom soup and one can of water, and bake in a moderate oven until tender.

Net folded prior to banding

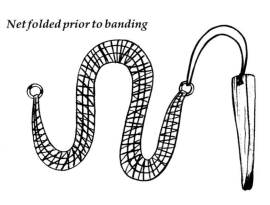

Elastic band secures fold

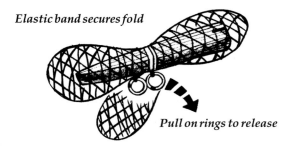

Pull on rings to release

A purse net folded as shown is ready for action simply by pulling on the rings.

CHAPTER 7

Having learned a lot during my apprenticeship as a rabbiting man, I also discovered a great deal about hares and how to deal with them in reasonable numbers. It would be silly to suggest that the rabbit would not head my list of favourite quarry because everyone who knows me is well aware of this. On the other hand, of course, in the business of learning about rabbits, one does gain some knowledge of hares as well and it appears to me that when there is a decline in the hare population, the rabbit population increases and vice-versa. I do not know whether this applies to other parts of the country or not, but it is just my experience.

I learned how to recognise a hare form, but I must admit that I never reached the stage when I was able to kill a crouching hare in its form with a stick or catapult as I had so often done with rabbits. As I progressed with my old single-barrelled shotgun, I learned how to take rabbits on the run, as well as shooting them for the pot when they were squatting, as I had been wont to do. I also learned the art of squeaking a rabbit so that its ears popped up and presented me with a better target. This applied to the hunting of hares as well and I squawked rather than squeaked and eventually had the hares, at certain times of the year, coming towards me at full gallop. It was a most fascinating experience and one that I still enjoy doing today, just for the devil of it, not necessarily to kill the quarry. It obviously works best at Mad March Hare time, when the jack hares are seeking females, and when one comes running towards the sound it is generally a jack hare. Many times I have rested the rifle against a five-barred gate and executed a clean head-shot after calling a hare to me. I have even hidden in a ditch, called a hare to me, shot it and then another hare has appeared from nowhere and tried to mate with it in its death throes. I could easily have killed that one, too, but I thought that was not playing the game!

I suppose I have shot more hares with a single-shot rifle than I have with a shotgun, for the simple reason that the targets have always been better presented for the rifle, but I have also taken many hares without pressing a trigger or shooting in any way, shape or form.

There was one huge field known as "The Hare Field" which has produced for me, over the years, many hares for the pot. I used to call it the Airfield because of my Buckinghamshire accent. Afterwards everybody always referred to it as the Airfield, though it took me some time to realise that it was hares, not aircraft, for which it was famed!

It was a vast field and it took ages to walk round, but in those days long walks of several miles meant little to me as long as the end product was forthcoming. It had two gates and several gaps in the hedge to which a walked-up hare would run as its escape route. What we used to do was carry several rolled-up newspapers and a ball of string and then stretch a piece of newspaper across a tied-up string in the gaps in the hedgerows. This would deter any hare from bolting through its normal escape route and I have often seen a number of them refuse several gaps and then head towards one of the gates. Of course, that gateway was already primed with a gate-net, which was deadly as far as our quarry was concerned.

There is another way I was taught to catch hares with a gate-net but without setting it in the correct manner. That was by laying the top string on to the gate top and weighing it down with two half bricks, then tying the two cords into the hedgerow. A running hare will not notice the net stretched across the gate and the more it is caught up the harder it will try to push its way forward. In doing so it dislodges the bricks and the hare is ensnared. Gateways in Buckinghamshire are often strengthened by hard core and half bricks were readily on hand!

There was a poacher many years ago who ridiculed me for nominating this method as a means of catching hares. Little enough did he know, for this idea, taught to me by an old countryman, worked and worked well. The other way of setting a net, of course, was to peg it and stake it down in the fashion of a long-net, about eight yards in front of the gate, to catch a hare in the normal way. There was nothing really clever about it.

I always enjoyed coursing a hare with a running dog, either a greyhound or a lurcher. I get pleasure from watching the chase whether the hare is caught or not. A single dog seldom succeeds. It usually takes two, one to head the hare, and one to catch it. It is most interesting to see an arrogant hare (and they are arrogant creatures) simply turn its head, note that it is being caught up, change up a gear, and calmly avoid the dog chasing it. That, to me, is a contest well worth watching and I don't care whether the hare escapes or not. I have no conscience about it and I think that a hare caught thus is probably better than one that is walked up and shot. However, today, under the absurd Hunting Bill, coursing hares is no longer permitted.

The most hares I ever took in a day were five. I realise, of course, that this number could be vastly exceeded by one Gun on a driven hare shoot when the bag at the end of the day might be 200 or more hares, but I was shooting for the pot at the time. There were five of us involved and so it worked out very well. I was standing on the edge of a wood, about a quarter of a mile from a long hedgerow my companions were working, in the hopes of putting up an odd pheasant. However, they must have disturbed several hares because five came at me headlong. I took them well forward and all were head-shot, destined for the pot.

Is there any dish more tasty than jugged hare? My mother used to chop the hare into portions and place them in an old stone pickle jar, put a saucer on top and leave it in the kitchen range all night so that, by the next morning, the meat was well-cooked and literally falling off the bones. I have never tasted better jugged hare, but today I tend to cut off the meat for sausages and use the bones for stock. Fried with a little really fat pork, there is no better tasting sausage, in my opinion.

I have many times sat up in an old hay-loft with my gun by my side and watched the cavortings of the Mad March hares, as they boxed and danced in front of me. I could have shot any one of them at my leisure but it was more fun just watching. I have sent an old labrador into a crowd of boxing hares and watched him wonder what he was supposed to do next, surrounded as he was by the animals. He hardly knew which one to chase!

I tend not to regard hare as game but prefer to get rid of all the surplus blood and leave the carcass in salt water for a couple of days to remove any trace of game flavour. I have, in fact, treated them more or less like rabbits for any number of years. I've also cooked rabbit and hare together so that there has been, apart from the colour and texture of the meat, little to choose between the flavour of the two.

I would be fibbing if I said that rabbits were not number one on my quarry list but I still enjoy hunting hares and I place them as a close second.

HARE CASSEROLE

Put joints of hare into a casserole dish. Fry diced onions, carrots and celery in hot butter or fat, dust with flour and cook until brown. Place the vegetables on top of the hare portions, cover with well-seasoned stock, add sliced tomatoes, a little chopped green pepper and a pinch of mixed herbs. Cook slowly in a covered dish until the gravy is thick and the meat falling off the bones. Adjust the seasoning and serve. The left-overs, when cold, can be separated from the bones, packed into waxed cartons and deep-frozen for future quick meals.

CHAPTER 8

When I was younger and had a lot of enthusiastic ferreting friends, we took great delight in attacking a very big infestation of rabbits with the aim of clearing the lot in one big effort. It was a noisy adventure! There was nothing very clever about it for nothing was sacred. The hedgerow had to go, the fences had to come down, but at least the farmer understood the situation, for the damage being inflicted on his land by the hordes of rabbits was costing him a fortune. We started at one end of a big hedgerow and ransacked it right the way through to the end, using the line ferret at the very end because that's where most of the rabbits had ended up. They, of course, had to be dug out, but that was par for the course. I am rather ashamed of these adventures now but at the time they seemed to be the thing to do.

On one occasion we tackled such a situation on a 1,000 acre farm which was roughly divided in two by a small stream, no more than six feet across. The difference between the two sides was quite remarkable. We decided that, on this occasion, we would probably have to use the softly-softly approach rather than the rabbiting gang's approach which left nothing standing. Two of us with a few ferrets and nets tackled the ground on the right-hand side of the stream but it was not a very successful arrangement. The ferrets bolted six rabbits, three of which were in an advanced stage of myxomatosis and obviously had to be killed and left. The dog managed to catch another pristine rabbit and we ended up by going home with a brace apiece which was all we could muster on that occasion.

However, the following week we decided to work the left-hand side of the stream to see if it was any different. Don't ask me why we did this. All I can say it was a whim and the rabbits were there to be killed. They were running around in large numbers and did not appear to be stricken with myxy. The hedgerow bury was too large to consider using only purse-nets. It was vast and encompassed a double hedge which, in days gone by, indicated a parish boundary. We had been instructed (which really means were allowed) to do our best to tackle the serious rabbit problem, but it was one of those situations in which two ferrets and 100 purse-nets were not really sufficient. This was a big-time effort that demanded special measures. I confess I do not look for such opportunities any more but, because I had a couple of willing supporters, I decided to give it a go. We could rustle up 210 purse-nets between us but we would have needed double that number to be in with a reasonable chance. However, we also had two gate-nets which, together, would set 25 yards, and we put these through the double hedge at the upwind end of the complex. Our strategy was simple enough in the circumstances. We purse-netted about every other hole to conserve our equipment, and figured that any rabbit bolting from an uncovered hole would be back-netted when it sought sanctuary down another. This is a good ploy when nets are in short supply and, although nothing is ever guaranteed, it works most of the time. The exception, of course, is the rabbit that breaks from the bury and heads away at right angles over open country. Most bolting rabbits, though, run up or down a hedgerow and should obviously be encouraged to take the route to the set "insurance" stop net at the far end.

Generally speaking, rabbits in large, multi-holed, hedgerow complexes tend to play tag with ferrets hunting underground. They will vacate an obviously un-netted hole - one which their natural caution tells them is safe - and dive quickly down an adjacent one. If that one has been covered, the game of tag is over as the quarry is neatly back-netted. With only every other hole netted as many rabbits are caught going in as are caught running out. Even if both holes selected are uncovered, no harm is done. The quarry is still available! It is essential, however, to remain silent when rabbits duck and dive in this fashion. This is why I do not want frantic, yapping terriers, which go berserk at the sight of a rabbit, anywhere near my area of work.

Terrier lovers, this is my own personal opinion and does not detract from my liking for your dogs. Your terrier may not misbehave. Yours

may not charge from hole to hole like a demented squirrel flitting from branch to branch in an oak tree. If so, you are to be congratulated, and I do so with genuine feeling. I have yet to see one so well trained, however, although I am assured they exist!

I have learned, over many years of practice, that once rabbits learn that all is not well above ground they do their best not to show any more. The spoken voice, a waving arm or a barking dog will quickly deter rabbits from bolting and guarantee a miserable dig!

Another way of conserving purse-nets is to set them in a progressive "leapfrog" pattern. Working from the downwind end to the stop-net upwind, use up all the available purse-nets as far as they will go, and enter ferrets so that rabbits will be more or less be obliged to head upwind. If they make a clean break they may be caught in the stop net. If they play tag, they may be back-netted or reach comparative safety by diving down the un-netted end of the complex. However, it is hardly possible to achieve this kind of drive forward unless several ferrets are put to work.

The simplest strategy is to let the advance continue but to hold a single ferret in reserve to deal with quarry that manages to back-track. This happens often enough and, even with reserves in use, there is no guarantee that the warren complex will be completely exploited.

This is skilful ferreting and field-craft at its best. When rabbits have been pushed forward and the first say 10 sets are "redundant", these have to be picked up, carried forward in silence, and set to continue where the others ran out originally. If a hole is difficult to net or would require a great deal of disturbance to do so, it is better left alone. Better to risk the odd escapee than to end up with reluctant rabbits backed up in numbers at the end of the hunt because of their fear of vacating.

On the day in question, because of the enormity of the task ahead, we used eight jill ferrets with two big hobs on standby. We kept four jills working underground at any one time and when one appeared in confusion above ground we rested her and sent down a relief. It proved unnecessary to use the hobs. I spent much of my time paunching, legging and hanging prime rabbits as they were dispatched, but I also covered possible escape routes and managed to grab a couple of bewildered tail-enders.

"You'll have thirty rabbits by this afternoon," said the local lurcher man who came to watch the proceedings. "You did right to make an early start. Too many ferreters leave it too late and get lie-ups after lunch."

How right he was! No-one in his right mind would tackle a complex such as this other than at crack of dawn. It becomes harder for me each year and soon it will be too hard, but you must have time to tackle big jobs!

The amount of labour involved might have warranted more quarry than we actually caught but I was happy to settle for 31 prime rabbits all bolted.

And if you don't believe that was sheer, sporting pleasure, you are not truly a fan of ferrets or ferreting. I've had better days but I'll settle for one like that any time!

RABBIT PIE I

To make a good rabbit pie, first stew the rabbit with onions and carrots.

Thicken the stock with a brown roux, place all in a pie dish and cover with short-crust pastry. Glaze the surface with egg and bake until the pastry is cooked.

RABBIT PIE II

1 rabbit
½lb bacon or pickled pork
½lb beefsteak
½ pint stock
Salt and pepper
Short-crust or puff pastry

Divide the rabbit into small joints, cut the beef into small thin slices, and dice the pork. Place these ingredients in layers in a pie-dish, season each layer liberally with salt and pepper, and three-quarters fill the dish with stock made from the rabbit bones. Cover with pastry, bake for 1¾-2 hours in a brisk oven until the pastry has risen and set, and afterwards more slowly. Before serving, add the remainder of the hot stock to the pie. When the pie is intended to be eaten cold, forcemeat balls and hard-boiled eggs will be found an improvement, and the appearance may be improved by brushing it over with yolk of egg when three-quarters baked.

CHAPTER 9

Shortly before the outbreak of the Second World War I became frustrated by the situation in Britain and, to fulfil my life-long urge to travel, I joined the Royal Tank Corps. Early in January 1938 I found myself engaged in the long, long walk from Wool Station to the camp at Bovington, Dorset. I was cold and wet and thoroughly miserable, and wondered what on earth I had done. However, I soon settled down into the Army routine and eventually volunteered for Foreign Service in 1939. I arrived in Egypt in July of that year and progressed from there, which was just as well because it meant that I missed Dunkirk and all its horrors. I was in Egypt when war was declared and was up at the front line the moment Italy came into the war.

This was no longer rabbiting territory or rabbiting country, and no longer a time to think about my former days of sport. But there were the odd jack rabbits in the Western Desert and for several years I travelled up and down, obeying the instructions of the various Generals who decided which or what way I was supposed to go. We did, over the years, take a few jack rabbits with catapult or rifle or various other means. It was not strictly rabbiting but to kill a jack rabbit and to eat it round a very mild campfire was a welcome change from the never-ending supply of bully beef. I came back to England in time for D-Day but, thankfully, was not involved in the invasion. I went to France a short while afterwards when everything had quietened down and I was happy to land on the beach without problems.

Eventually, after a variety of soldiering adventures I found myself back in England, after having been slightly burnt. I ended up at Lunecliffe Camp just outside Lancaster with the Border Regiment and there I met Tommy Arkwright who was an absolute dyed-in-the-wool shooting man and very, very keen on rabbits. He had a wife in Fleetwood and, so too did I, because I had squeezed in the time to marry the girl who became my wife for over sixty years, so we cycled the route across Pilling Sands to see our wives at every opportunity.

As soon as we were finished in camp we went looking for rabbits or the odd pheasant or two which lay around the camp where we were stationed. Our old single-barrelled shotguns stood us in good stead and we took our toll of the game around that particular area. Whether we were legally entitled to do so I have no idea but as soldiers we were allowed to carry guns, and so we took advantage of the sporting opportunities around the various fields on the huge estate.

Whilst there I met a man whose name completely escapes me but who was the Pest Officer for Lancashire, as far as I remember. He was brilliant at catching rabbits, mostly trapping above ground and by running a long-net. Now long-netting was very important to me because I had learned quite a bit about this particular skill in the south, and, by the grace of God, the Pest Officer allowed me to accompany him. I was not happy with catching rabbits in gin-traps (as they are still called) above ground because they were, to my thinking, very cruel.

I remember, however, one night in particular with the long-net. I went out with him to set a 100-yard net. He was exceptionally good at picking up and re-laying it. I have never been able to do it more than twice myself but on this particular night he ran it five times and we killed nearly 100 rabbits.

So much rubbish is written about long-nets that it makes me cross even to read it, especially when people talk about catching hundreds and hundreds of rabbits in a long-net. It irritates me because I know that a 100-yard long net will accommodate, if you are lucky, 20 rabbits, and a score of rabbits in one net is incredible because it means that they have to be spread out between the 10-stake setting. That's two rabbits per 10 yards and how often this happens is just too rare to contemplate.

However, on this occasion we picked up 93 rabbits and I remember gutting, hocking and hanging them on tree branches away from the creatures of the night so that they were ready to be picked up by pony and trap the next morning. It was one of the most incredible rabbiting experiences of my life and I learned such a lot on that occasion. It stood me in good stead, for many years to come, on less productive areas in the south and around Buckinghamshire, which is my home territory.

When we were at Lunecliffe, Tommy and I used to travel to the

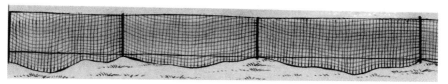

Lune Estuary in the hope that we could bag a duck for the table with our single-barreled guns. More often we spent our spare time hunting rabbits with an old stray dog which was always keen to join us because he was obviously a hunter. He used to turn rabbits out of the hedge and we used to shoot them.

On one occasion our regiment went to the local barracks to enjoy a Christmas dinner. When everybody was off duty Tommy and I took our guns, a ferret, a few nets, our fishing rods and sallied forth in the early hours of the morning. We killed several rabbits, caught a pike and shot a pheasant. It was a wonderful day's sport but when we came back everybody in the camp was still half-merry as a result of the camp dinner and told us what we had missed. Little did they know that we had had a much better experience than they had - in my opinion!

So I continued my rabbiting and at the same time I learned a lot more about hares and the general countryside in the north; knowledge which I was able to apply after I was demobilized and returned south to home and Aylesbury. Two years later my young daughter was born and soon learned to live on such delectable items as moorhen, rabbits and game because meat rationing was then in operation. However, she had a wonderful growing up time and the experience did her no harm. Little did she know that she was being fed better, because of my rabbiting experiences, than anybody else in the area. She realised that in due course though and now, in my 85th year as I write, and as I await the onset of my 60th wedding anniversary and her arrival from her new home in Australia, she has asked if we may possibly have rabbit pie on several occasions during her stay. She need ask no further!

I remember, too, on one occasion around Lunecliffe retrieving a rabbit from one of the local poaching cats. It had killed the rabbit and had sucked the jugular dry, then departed in a hurry as I approached. I saw that it was a clean-killed rabbit and took it back to the camp for the table.

It is, perhaps, not quite so well known that any rabbit killed by a stoat, a weasel or a domesticated cat loses its blood in the process and becomes a much whiter and more palatable dish, so I have always been pleased to discover rabbits which have been caught and killed by a stoat or a weasel.

I once shot a running rabbit with my 12-bore single barrel in the company of a Sergeant who was new to the experience. The rabbit jumped up in front of me, ran to the right, and I shot it. Immediately it rolled over, stone dead, and when I came to pick it up it had, I swear, every single pellet in the cartridge, plus the wad and odd bits of paper which had been involved in the loading of my home-made cartridges, embedded in its head. What had happened is that the cartridge contents had balled up, as they rarely but occasionally do, and my shot had been so remarkably lucky that the whole lot had hit the rabbit in the head. It was one of the best shots that I have ever made in my life but, of course, it was sheer luck.

Back home at Aylesbury I was introduced by my father to one Ralph Rayner, who was one of the finest rabbit shots that I have ever seen and has only recently died at the age of 96. He was a wonderful man who understood rabbits inside and out and who taught me so much. However, I have to say that some of what he told me was wrong and I learned, as the years progressed, to sift the wheat from the chaff and eventually to become a rabbiting man.

RABBIT POT ROAST

Cut up two rabbits, flour and brown them in an iron skillet in bacon fat. Place browned pieces into an iron pot, and add about a quart of water, a splash of cider vinegar, a little piece of bay leaf, a slice of onion, salt, and an egg-sized lump of country butter. Simmer this slowly till the meat falls off the bones, and then pick out the bones. About half an hour before supper, stir in some flour and milk thickening. Bootiful!

CHAPTER 10

When I first met Paddy McCoy I could tell that he was a rabbiting man with a purpose. His one simple aim in life was to enjoy his rabbiting and not to worry too much about putting quarry in the bag. He certainly was not into rabbit clearance.

Paddy had two whippets. They were well-trained, well-behaved, and knew exactly what to do. Very often I used to join him in the cold winter weeks and I would always take a couple of loose ferrets and a hob liner just in case they were needed. The idea was, as Paddy always said, to let the dogs do the work, leave them to it and not interfere with them. He used to like working open buries, that is to say buries in the open field, rather than the hedgerow buries. However, when he worked the hedgerows he put a whippet on either side and liked to have someone else with him so that both sides of the hedgerow were covered. There was no shooting and no netting. It was simply a case of letting the ferrets bolt the rabbits and leave the rest to the whippets. Believe me, they really knew what they were supposed to do.

Very few rabbits escaped. The whippets were very, very quick off the mark and occasionally they would close up together, one acting as a header dog and the other doing the catching. Each individual whippet was, however, capable of catching a rabbit in its own right. We simply put loose ferrets in and let them run around while we kept well back and left the bolting quarry to make a break for it. Each time a rabbit was chased by the whippets, it was successfully harvested. It was poetry in motion, and though it was a form of sport not perhaps enjoyed by everyone, it was a most enjoyable exercise.

I remember working an in-field bury on one particular morning when seven rabbits broke for cover; each was caught by the whippets, and three more ended up in a dead-end in a shallow part of the complex. These were easily dug and brought our total up to ten rabbits. Ten rabbits without a gun or a net is, I think, a very respectable result for a morning's work. It was not rabbit clearance but it certainly was exciting.

Another form of rabbiting which I have enjoyed, even though not directly involved, is hunting with hawks. I have accompanied some of the finest field sportsmen I have ever known, watching them fly their marvellous birds to rabbits bolted by ferrets. The falconers that I have hunted with are all members of the Hawking Society and have among their membership John Buckner, Laurie Workman, Adrian Williams and many others who love their birds, breed new stock and work them to ferrets for rabbits during the winter months. They thoroughly enjoy this old-fashioned, traditional and so exciting field sport. They will probably accept the fact that flying hawks to bolted rabbits is not, strictly speaking, as efficient or as effective as some other methods, but simply watching these magnificent birds work to their natural quarry, with ferrets in the background, is something rather special.

The hawks used are goshawks, Harris hawks and red-tailed hawks. These last named are lumpy birds and have no fear of thick cover or any other interruption when flying to their quarry. They have strong feathers and are very hard birds. In fact, if they spot a rabbit in cover they will fly directly into a patch of briar or bramble and hold the rabbit down, which is more than can be said for other hawks, some of which are more careful and probably a little more on the delicate side.

My favourite species, of course, is the Harris hawk. I have been allowed to work with these many times and it is marvellous to watch those pristine birds follow and fly as their handlers' work them. I have watched a Harris hawk perch on a branch and wait and watch until a rabbit has appeared. It will not make its move until it is absolutely certain it can produce the goods.

Goshawks, too, are remarkable. Adrian Williams tells me the story of the day his goshawk, weighing much less than a pound-and-a-half, flew and tackled a rabbit, which weighed 4½lb, holding it firmly. That, I think, is something quite remarkable.

It is not an easy sport and sometimes the hawks fly in competition with each other. The Harris hawk always flies in the knowledge that it will be helped by another member of the family. They call it, I believe, "flying in cast", and if a hawk holds down a hare or a rabbit and cannot manage it, another hawk will come to assist it. I am completely fascinated by the whole procedure.

I think that rabbiting with hawks must be among the greatest of all field sports and I wish that I had known about it earlier and become a hawking man in my own right. It is too late now for me to consider that. On the other hand, I am fortunate to be invited out year after year by the hawking fraternity and to enjoy their sport and their generous hospitality.   I hope this may long continue.

The bond between the hawking man and his bird is obvious when he comes to lift a hawk holding down a rabbit. Some sleight of hand is involved as fresh meat is placed in front of the bird and the carcass is then stealthily slipped in to the retaining bag.

It is, to my way of thinking, a field sport with a difference. As far as I am concerned, these people, many of whom stem from South Wales, know what they are about and it is a great pleasure for me to watch them at work. This is not rabbit clearance but it is one of the most enjoyable forms of rabbiting in which I have participated during my long and rabbit-filled life.

RABBIT SUET PUDDING

Joint the rabbit, putting the head, neck, liver and kidneys aside, afterwards to be stewed for gravy. Roll rabbit portions in seasoned flour, place in a pudding basin lined with suet dough, with carrots, mushrooms and onions. Press down tightly. Cover with water or stock, seal with a pudding crust lid, cover with a cloth and steam for at least two hours. Stewing beef, kidneys or lean, uncooked ham, can be added if you wish.

Turn out the pudding on a hot dish and serve with gravy made from the head and other scraps.

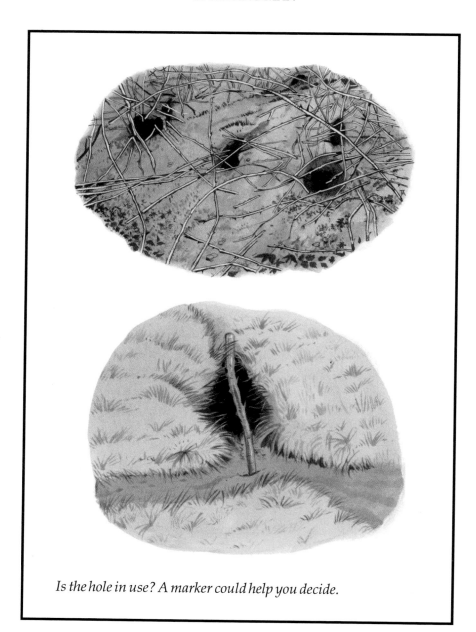

Is the hole in use? A marker could help you decide.

CHAPTER 11

Lamping has been mentioned only briefly but it is worth remembering that the use of the spotlight in the dark hours is one of the most deadly methods of catching rabbits. This is especially true in Australia where it is recognised as probably the most practical method of rabbit control.

There is a difference, of course, in the British and Australian situations. The rabbits in Australia are located in wide open areas with no nearby hedgerows and, as a result, they venture farther from the warren in order to exploit feeding areas, so it is possible to tackle them with a four-wheel-drive, a lamp operator and a simple one-shot rifle.

In England we tend to use a red filter over the lens of the spotlight so that the rabbit is lit up but doesn't realise it! It continues to feed and can be shot where it sits. In Australia the red filter is not used, as far as I know. The idea of the spotlight in that country is to use one as powerful as possible to confuse and temporarily blind the rabbits so that they remain seated. It is even possible, and I have mentioned it before, to run and pick up rabbits with one's bare hands because, dazzled by the strong beam, they don't know exactly where you are. It's not really practical to follow this procedure in England for here most of the rabbits are near to hedgerow buries and have to be taken as quickly as possible. The best way to do that is, I feel, by using the red light.

We have portable units with a satchel bag carrying the battery, and a trigger on the spotlight so that, if we wish, we can walk about and shoot without the need to use a four-wheel-drive truck. It is, though, not as efficient because much less ground can be covered in search of quarry.

Many operators, of course, use running dogs with the lamp and those can have remarkable success in areas where rabbits are widespread. Their lurchers or running dogs are not troubled by the lamp but follow the beam and pick up the quarry in the light itself.

Those who practise this regularly tell me that it is very unwise to hunt more often than once a week because, they say, it wears the dog out and renders it incapable of working.

Confusing rabbits in a strong spotlight beam does not always work. Many rabbits run at the first sign of being lit up and make for shelter immediately. It is very noticeable, however, that for some reason (and I don't pretend to understand why) we can often drive a four-wheel-drive vehicle right up to the rabbit itself without always causing it any alarm. I would have thought that the noise of the engine would have frightened it but this seldom happens. It is a simple way of approaching and getting into close range.

Many years ago I taped a long, strong torch to the side of my shotgun and was able to take care of many rabbits in this fashion. It was simple enough but, of course, in those days there were many more around to be caught. I do not think the method would work so well today.

The powerful spotlight with a red lens may also be used as an extension to an evening's warren shooting. Everyone knows, or should know by now, that the approach to the warren is made downwind so that the human scent is not driven towards the bury. However, there are times when the rabbits stubbornly refuse to come out during the summer evening hours. This is a selective kind of shooting. One does not wish to kill pregnant does, nor to shoot very young rabbits running around. So it is also a waiting game. We sit and wait until a half-grown rabbit appears and then shoot it. If we are lucky, we may get a couple. These are prime quarry and well worth the wait. Waiting can, however, be a tedious game when the rabbits seem to be well aware that all is not well above ground. The spotlight and red lens can then be put to good use to extend the evening shooting into the dark hours.

Despite it being a spotlight, it does tend to illuminate quite an area on the warren and sitting there shortly after dark with a rifle with telescopic sights can result in several rabbits being taken which would otherwise be missed.

RABBIT IN FOIL

Place rabbit portions on a sheet of foil, dot with lard and smother with diced ham, bacon or pork, and chopped onions. Sprinkle with salt, pepper and sage, wrap into a parcel and cook for about one hour in a hot oven. Before serving, open up the foil to allow the contents to crisp.

Or you could even - would you believe? double-wrap it and cook it in the ash pan under the living room fire!

CHAPTER 12

We do not hear much these days about the number of rabbits hauled out of a dead end or stop when they have constantly refused to bolt. This was a common occurrence in the days before myxomatosis and the many rabbits that might be found in a dead end, when using the line ferret, were unbelievable.

We were discussing this one evening around a pint of beer. Several of us who are interested in fishing and ferrets had got together and were having a quiet drink. We were talking about those, shall we say, "good old days" when rabbits did not bolt freely but were often located in large numbers at a dead end.

Strangely enough, towards the end of one rabbiting season, Alec Martin, my partner, and I located a rabbit haunt underneath a rotten tree which only held two holes, one entrance and one exit. We put in a collared jill and let her roam around but the rabbits would not bolt. We knew there was more than one in there and the electronic locator showed that the jill was laid up, however many rabbits there were.

There often comes a time when the locator and the collar do not work as well as the good old line ferret. I tell you this because, when we dug down where the signal showed the ferret was located, we encountered underground roots and branches which made digging more or less impossible. So, as she had herded the rabbits up to a dead end, I put in the old hob liner and quickly removed the collared jill from the rabbit she was latched on to. That is what a line ferret does, of course. It drives the jill off and takes over the quarry for himself.

From then on it was not a question of one, but several digs. I located the line in different situations and followed this through with a flexible stick. Eventually I went round the roots and back towards the entrance where I started. It took three digs but I was able to locate the rabbits under the roots at the dead end, or stop, in the fullness of time. There were, in fact, seven rabbits! That is something which I have not experienced for many years, indeed since myxomatosis put paid to most of our sport for a period.

When I started rabbiting again, after the disease, I borrowed a ferret because I didn't have any of my own and the owner said he would be happier if I used the creature on a line. This did not bother me because the bury I intended to work was not very large. I think his ferret was a pet and he was afraid of losing him, so I did his bidding, lined him up and proceeded to work with him to the best of my ability. On that particular day, in a small bury, we located five rabbits in one dead end, and this really and truly started me off on the ferreting game once more. Having pulled out the rabbits, one after the other, I was stirred into further action, bought more ferrets and started my own line of stock. The horrors of myxomatosis were now a memory, though there were still regular outbreaks, and rabbits were once again spreading throughout the countryside. Later on, when I met

Malcolm Baldwin, we put our stocks together to create a line of quiet, very active and deadly ferrets, and we used these for well over twenty years.

Before myxomatosis, on one occasion I managed to extract no fewer than sixteen rabbits from one dead end or stop. This, to me, was absolutely incredible and yet it was nothing compared with the number of rabbits my old friend Ralph Raynor extracted from a very shallow mid-field bury one January morning. Nowhere were the buries more than six inches deep and they could be clawed out by hand. Believe it or not, Ralph pulled out some 33 rabbits, all bunched up in one dead end. Some of them had already been killed by the line ferret but the others were still lively and kicking. This was something we often experienced during the days of line ferreting, occasional hedgerow poaching and the general rabbiting which we used to practise, though not usually in such numbers.

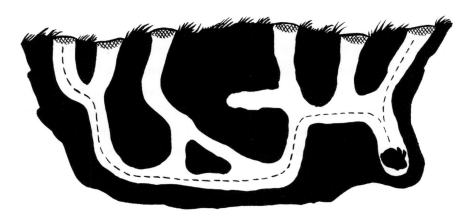

Location using a line ferret. By listening for the ferret a shorter distance and less digging may be involved.

It was our policy on many occasions to block in the rabbit holes in an outlying field and crouch in the ditches where we could work unseen. Using the line ferret we would follow the line to dig out those bunnies which we intentionally bunched up into a dead end. This was certainly a very different form of ferreting to that practised today. I am not too sure whether it was good or bad. The only thing was that the more we dug, the fewer rabbits we were able to bolt.

I once extracted nine rabbits from a single hole bury which had no exit, merely an entrance. I achieved this simply by walking around and driving the rabbits into the one entrance hole. They all bunched up so that I could use a line ferret and picked them all out of the dead end. On another occasion, I located two dead ends and took five out of one and four out of the other.

Ferreting has changed, there is no doubt about that, but the old days and the old ways seemed, to me, to be quite remarkable. The more I went ferreting the more I learned.

To tell the honest truth, the days when we were able to collect bolted rabbits neatly in the purse-net were exceptional rather than normal. In a way, although it sounds rather silly, there was not quite so much excitement involved as there was in digging down and finding several at the end of a stop. It was entirely different, of course. Today there are not the numbers of rabbits about so I doubt if we shall ever go back to practising this way of ferreting any more.

The electronic collar and the locator both help to make sure that we do not waste too much time locating our rabbits, and when we do find them we have only the one dig, generally speaking, to come to terms with a carcase or a live rabbit. Nowadays I am happy to let the ferrets work the buries and bolt the rabbits as much as possible, but I must admit that much of the real enthusiasm and excitement has gone.

When we used to work from one end of the hedgerow to another and gradually bunch the rabbits into one big dead end before we dug out and took the lot, it was a different procedure. I suppose in those days we would have had it no other way. Today I am prepared to change my mind and hope for the bolters rather than those which have to be dug! The locator makes life somewhat easier!

BAKED RABBIT IN SAUCE

Lay portions of rabbit in a casserole dish. Smother with chopped carrots and onions, season and add a tin of mushroom soup or a suitable cook-in sauce. Cook slowly in the oven. The dish can be covered with grated cheese or sliced potatoes if you wish.

CHAPTER 13

Rabbit behaviour had, so I believed, changed in recent years and I conjured up a theory that more and more rabbits were venturing into standing corn and remaining there until the harvest. There had been signs, as far as I could tell, that recently an increasing number of rabbits were lying out rather than burrowing underground, and I began to wonder whether this was the result of three factors - standing corn, set-aside and myxomatosis.

My theory was simple enough. Rabbits were now moving in small numbers into the standing corn in the summer or taking advantage of the set-aside scrub fields in order to remain above ground and so avoid the underground fleas which spread the *myxoma* virus. This made, in my view, a perfectly logical case, for I have not seen quite so many myxomatosis-stricken rabbits in recent years. There have been fewer carcasses on the road, and not so many rabbits by the roadside in prime healthy condition, and this led me to suppose that there were other options. Set-aside fields and the cornfields now offered, I concluded, a refuge to rabbits seeking respite from the dreaded disease.

Despite all we reckon to know about rabbits, strategically and tactically, they are invariably one step ahead of us and will always beat us. Their numbers are down nowadays due to disease and heavy predation, but they are still always around in numbers enough to cause some farmers problems. It was easy, therefore, to come to the conclusion that more rabbits were remaining above ground than were digging underground during the months of summer. I suppose it was wishful thinking on my part but you have to follow a theory to its logical conclusion and this seemed about right to me.

In 2004, however, we did not take part in our usual light-hearted harvest shoot for the simple reason that there was no harvesting. The corn, which we expected the rabbits to be in, was left standing. It was saturated and flattened in many places and I couldn't for the life of me imagine many rabbits wishing to remain under cover in those conditions.

The opportunities for a harvest shoot vary from year to year

On the other hand, further south, a couple of friends killed a few rabbits and drove out a fox during the last few turns of the combine harvester. Their harvest was earlier, the ground was drier and sandier, and so, understandably, there was a difference between their rabbits in sand and ours in clay.

Of late, however, because of our particularly wet seasons, fewer rabbits have been lying out and my theory has been demolished. Now there are signs that an increasing number of rabbits are going to ground and the first few days of the unofficial rabbiting/ferreting season confirm this again. The harvest, nowadays, generally seems to take place earlier each year and I have even heard of ferreters starting work in August! This was unheard of a few years ago, for we usually waited until the first few frosts have touched the countryside before venturing forth with the ferrets. However, it was also our policy to seek the rabbits that had gone to ground immediately after the harvest had been cut. These were our "harvest" quarry!

I have noticed, though, that one or two forms are beginning to show up again and that there is the odd rabbit lying out in long grass forms in the set-aside territory. Our rabbits may be changing their habits a little

Rabbit in a form

to adapt to altering weather and climate conditions, however we shall never know the true reason for rabbits changing their ways of life but it is as well that they do.

An example of rabbits lying out is in the woodland or covert situation. The shallow buries they once used in the woodlands are no longer with us but they seem to be occupying great overhangs of bramble and heavy undergrowth. Again I wonder whether this has something to do with the *myxoma* virus, and it certainly makes a difference when hunting them. Rabbits in small, shallow, underground buries can be netted and ferreted without problems but when they are lying up under heavy undergrowth they are not quite so vulnerable.

We may never again shoot rabbits lying out as we used to before myxomatosis days but it is nice to think that perhaps (and I say "perhaps") a few of the rabbits may again be choosing to lie out rather than to burrow underground. This makes for good walked-up shooting on days when the rabbit is not essentially the number one quarry but can be supplemented with game such as pheasants, partridges and, of course, the odd duck.

When rabbits were lying thick on the ground, pheasants were uncommon birds and only occasionally featured in our walked-up shoots. Today almost every double hedge offers a good opportunity for a flushed bird for reared pheasants are found countrywide, and spread into the most unlikely spots.

My theory about above-ground rabbits was knocked for six because of a long, wet summer, but who knows what next year will bring? It may produce an entire reversal of the situation so that at least some rabbits will have reverted back to becoming above-ground dwellers. Either way it makes very little difference because they can be hunted in both situations, but I believe variety is the spice of life and it is encouraging to see one's theories coming almost to fruition. I shall follow the situation with interest and I hope I never stop thinking! Rabbiting demands a study of strategy as well as tactics and will always be a part of the rabbiting man's approach. That is one of my reasons for its serious study.

RABBIT CREAM-HORN

Brush the hind legs of a young, tender rabbit with French mustard and a little pepper and salt. Cut strips of puff pastry about ¾in wide and spiral them around the legs in "cream horn" fashion. Then brush with egg glaze and cook at 425°F until the pastry rises and browns, reducing the heat to 350°F until the rabbit is tender.

BAKED RABBIT WITH FORCEMEAT

Fully enclose the hind legs of several young rabbits in a covering of forcemeat, e.g. sage and onion stuffing. Lay them separately in a baking dish and cover with bacon rashers. Bake slowly for about 1½ hours, testing with a fork, if necessary, to see if the rabbit is tender.

BAKED WHOLE RABBIT (AMERICAN STYLE)

Soak the rabbit overnight in water and vinegar. Drain off, split open the breast cavity and press flat in a baking dish. Add fried onions, a little diced green pepper, finely-chopped mushrooms and about 1 teaspoonful of brown sugar.Cover with a rich white sauce and bake in a moderate oven until tender.

CHAPTER 14

Hunting rabbits in Australia can in many respects be likened to hunting rabbits in England, but there are some differences with regard to time and temperature. It is of no use hunting rabbits during the summer in England because they are pregnant and milk-bound. In Australia, however, the heat and dryness of the situation ensures that the doe rabbits have no milk. They do not breed during the summer but wait until the winter when there is more moisture. Therefore, rabbit hunting takes place in the heat of the summer and that can be pretty gruesome and very tiring.

For the most part rabbits are hunted at night with a four-wheel drive vehicle and an automatic rifle. They are great wanderers and they leave the bury to go in search of food for quite a way so hunting them in the dark means, generally speaking, that they have no escape holes. Hunting rabbits with a spotlight is just that little bit different in Australia. They are simply fooled and bamboozled due to the strength of the spot-lamp. In my experience, as I have mentioned before, they are not hunted with red filters as they are in England. It is just a question of keeping them in the spotlight, transfixed, and shooting them where they sit. This can take place over a number of hours and the coolness of the night makes it a very pleasant way of hunting.

The only other method that I know is ferreting, which means an entirely different approach from that used in England. Warrens are created in the most desolate of areas and can number up to 100 or more holes. Rabbits remain underground during the heat of the day and venture forth to feed at night in an area which is devoted to feeding rather than a living area.

In the fierce heat of the Australian outback, or bush country, it is policy, generally speaking, to tip the ferrets in, let them run willy-nilly from hole to hole, and then shoot the rabbits as they bolt. In Australia they seem not to pop from hole to hole when chased by a ferret but make a clean break for it and offer very good sporting targets.

The fact that these warrens are areas accommodating very free bolters is established by the fact that they are never dug. They become basically "no-dig areas". Therefore we can say that either the rabbits bolt because the area is not dug or that the area is not dug because the rabbits bolt freely. In my opinion, it all boils down to the fact that these warrens are vast and accommodate large numbers of rabbits which are never reduced to creating dead-ends, stops and non-escape areas as a result of constant digging. The reason that these areas are not dug, if we tell the truth, is because they are very deep, vast and accommodate large numbers of rabbits and they are also home to creatures such as tiger snakes and other nasties which one can well do without meeting. Anyone who gropes around in the darkness in an area likely to hold tiger snakes is, in my estimation, asking for trouble, but it works out very well in the long run. Rabbits are quickly and easily dispatched, with few problems.

Rabbiting in Australia normally has to incorporate an overnight stay. Usually these vast outback areas are far from built-up areas and we find ourselves obliged to travel many miles to reach the rabbiting areas. It is hardly worthwhile trying to do it in one day and so we tend to make a camping experience of it, which, of course, is delightful.

Camps are established, wind-breaks are made and, generally speaking, they are close to one of the rabbit warrens we intend to tackle. It is always an enjoyable experience to camp out overnight in search of Australian rabbits because it allows us to ferret during the daytime and go lamping during the night. In between times, we simply have to crawl into bed in the camp and sleep until the next day.

When large numbers of rabbits are encountered, and the stay is to be overnight, ice boxes and cooler boxes are taken to start the event. Ice bottles and bags of crushed ice are taken in large quantities because of the very hot situation. Once the day's rabbiting is over, and the night is cool, the rabbits are then skinned, gutted, portioned and placed into the cooler boxes full of ice ready to be taken home next day. It is demanding work but it is enjoyable. In the event that rabbits are to be hunted for one day only, it is a simple matter to take some iced water and some wet sacks in order to keep them in good condition. A one-day hunt will take care of many rabbits placed in wet hessian sacks. It is essential, however, at all times, to take plenty of drinking water, plenty of ice and plenty of sustenance to keep one going throughout the very hot day. It is not unpleasant at all, providing these contingencies are allowed for and no chances are taken.

One of the great enjoyments during an overnight stay is the various cook-outs at the end of the session. Strangely enough, as I've mentioned before, the warm rabbits can be skinned, portioned and cooked in the Dutch oven to provide the evening meal after the day's work and evening chores are finished. It is a wonderfully relaxing time and one which is definitely part of a weekend's rabbiting in Australia.

Long-netting, generally speaking, is not practicable because there are no hedgerow buries in Australia that I am aware of, but it is possible to find a small warren involving, perhaps, fifty holes, and then run a long-net round it. It is a quick way to catch rabbits but I do not think that it can be compared with standing back and shooting them as they bolt.

One thing which is always noticeable, however, is that though the rabbits have no water their flesh is absolutely sweet and they can be cooked without any overnight cooling or hanging. Pellets are hard which signifies that they lack moisture, and yet the flesh is the best that I have tasted anywhere.

I earlier mentioned the fact that we don't dig for fear of meeting snakes, and I recall once seeing a ferret come face to face with a big tiger snake. It was absolutely panic-stricken and bolted from the warren as fast as a rabbit, and continued to run across the wild bushland so that we, who were taking care of it, had to run in order to catch it. It then had to be placed inside a cooler cage and kept in the shade until it settled. Even then it was reluctant to go down again on the same day.

Australian rabbits are, of course, originally from England and they have become very happy wanderers. A grazier named Thomas Austin imported two dozen rabbits in 1859 as he thought it would be nice to see a few bunnies hopping around and it might improve the sporting situation. He said that the introduction of a few rabbits could do little harm and might provide a touch of home. The rabbits, however, multiplied to such an extent that they spread throughout Victoria, New South Wales, Southern Queensland and South Australia. By 1894 they had crossed the Nullabor Plain and that in itself is absolutely remarkable. The Nullabor Plain is not, strictly-speaking, a desert but Nullabor means no trees. It is wild, sandy scrubland, and how those rabbits managed to acquire a living I can only guess. Many of them got into West Australia because rabbit hunters drove them towards the so-called rabbit-proof fence which has been erected where they piled one on top of each other until they were able to climb it. Those underneath were suffocated.

I can recall my dear old friend Ernie Chitty saying the numbers of rabbits were such that he once shot nine with a .22 rifle through the eye without so much as moving his feet. He received a penny apiece for rabbits at that time of year. Later the rabbits ate so much of the farmed crops that they became an emergency and a Royal Commission was held into the situation in 1904.

The rabbit-proof fence has been regarded by many as a joke but I can assure you that it is no such thing. It is an amazing piece of equipment which has done much to reduce the rabbit problem. I never cease to be amazed at the thought of what those men went through building the fence over several years. The intense heat and the overnight stays in a fly-ridden country must have been almost unbearable, but they stuck it out and they did the job. Today it is maintained by boundary riders who look after many miles of fence during their week's stay. Today, besides the rabbits, about 100,000 emus have gathered along the fence and they are capable of flattening it. Rats burrow underneath it and, of course, kangaroos are well known to be able to flatten fences. So it is a constant job to keep the fence erect in order to protect farm crops, as it does in a remarkable.

To describe a day's rabbiting with ferrets and later with a spotlight at night would, generally speaking, sound like a bragging exercise because so many rabbits are involved. I was not present on the occasion when Laurie Hateley and Bert Geddes took 167 rabbits with the ferrets in the daytime and then proceeded to the feed areas with the spotlight and four-wheel drive to make the number up to 200. Two hundred rabbits in a day is, I consider, pretty good going. I have been involved in some large catches myself but there have been others that were more interesting.

It is always nice to gather 50, 60 or even 100 rabbits in the course of a day's ferreting and I enjoyed it immensely. Putting purse-nets down is out of the question in that blistering heat and again it is just a question of standing back and shooting. I remember, however, one day when four foxes were killed during an ordinary rabbit hunt. Foxes and rabbits seem to live together happily in Australia as well as in England.

Rabbits have learned to adapt to Australian territory, which proves to me that the rabbit itself is a very versatile creature. It has become a happy wanderer in Australia though is no longer quite so numerous as it once was. The use of 1080 poison and spread of myxomatosis have taken care of a lot and they are now down to what I consider to be controllable numbers.

RABBIT SAUSAGE (AMERICAN STYLE)

Finely mince about 2 lb raw rabbit meat and 1 lb raw pork. Add 1 egg, a little sage, salt and paprika and 1 cupful of dry breadcrumbs. Mix together thoroughly, moistening with a little milk if too dry. Make into sausage or patty shapes. Fry in a heavy-duty pan or bake in a hot oven.

BARBECUE RABBIT (AMERICAN STYLE)

Place rabbit portions in pressure-cooker and cook briefly. Melt 1 oz. or so of butter in a heavy-duty pan and fry a couple of finely-chopped onions. Add 1 pint of tomato juice, 1 tablespoonful white vinegar, 1 tablespoonful brown sugar, salt, a pinch of cayenne pepper and a dash of Tabasco sauce. Pour over the cooked rabbit, cover with a lid and cook in a hot oven for about 15 minutes.

CHAPTER 15

I have had many hilarious attempts at long-netting during my long experience in the rabbiting field. Most of them have ended up with a brace or so bunnies or, at the most, half-a-dozen rabbits to take home after one single drop of the net. Big adventures involving several drops were not very often contemplated because I was not very good at it. I also liked to be home shortly after midnight because I had to go to work the next day.

I have already told of the night I spent with the professional rabbiter in Cumberland when the number of rabbits we caught was extraordinary. There have been a few other occasions which have involved several drops but which have not produced anything like that number of rabbits. Such a lot of rubbish is written about long-netting that I have no time to listen to it any more.

One of my favourite drops was on a farm where a long bury extended at least 100 yards and the rabbits had a 50-acre field in which to hop out and feed. The approach was fairly easy and all we had to do was creep quietly up (three of us) and set the net between the feeding field and the home bury. It is quite easy to do and all it required was stealth, low cunning, and quietness. Having set the net, the other two were sent to quarter the field and walk towards the long-net, and I was left to tend to any rabbits hitting it and becoming entangled.

This occasion was one of our better trips. I had put another long-net about 50 yards somewhere else in another field just for the sheer fun of doing so. I managed to dispatch 12 rabbits in the 100-yard-long net and when I went up to pick up the other net it had one rabbit in the mesh. That was 13 in a one-drop session. We were in the pub before it closed and home and in bed before midnight! That is what long-netting was all about as far as I was concerned.

For the most part, I had permission to run the long-net and to go rabbiting on several estates. It was not always so, however, and I confess to having broken the law on a few occasions in my early days. Following in my father's and uncles' footsteps, we followed the Hunt on Boxing Day, looking out for any good rabbit buries where we could drop the long-net and, I'm afraid, we tended to poach some areas where we did not have permission.

I had one old companion who would carry half the sleeve of an old jacket in his pocket with him. When he came to a barbed-wire fence we had to negotiate, he would not bother to try and climb it. He had a pair of pliers in his pocket and he would wrap the sleeve round the top wire and snip it through without making too much sound, and then left it. It wasn't fair and it was breaking the law I know but I was young, foolish and enthusiastic in those days. I have learned my lesson and am now much more moderate.

74

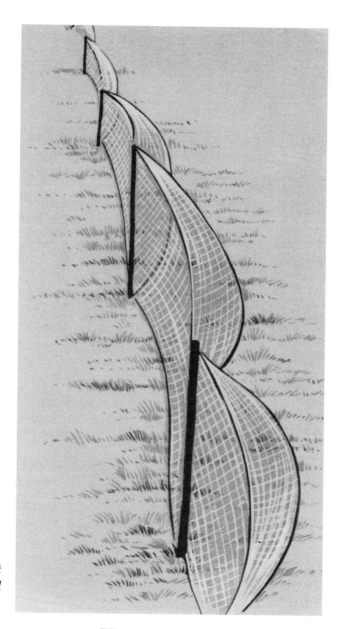

*A well set long net
with evenly spaced
poles*

I remember an occasion which seemed to me to be an absolutely ideal situation to drop a long-net. The wind was right, the night was dark and it was great to be out. We ran the long-net in front of a large bury which extended perhaps for 80 yards. The 100-yards of net covered any eventuality, and while I waited with hand on the top string, my companion walked the field and drove the rabbits towards the mesh. Every time there was a bump, I could feel it on the top string with my fingers and I went to look but there was no rabbit! It happened time and time again, and I became increasingly angry and frustrated. I couldn't understand what was going wrong. When we picked up the net, however, we found that the net had been set over one bolt hole that was left half exposed. The rabbits running towards home had apparently used this bolt-hole time and time again, hitting the bottom string as they sought cover. The whole net shook as it was expected to do and, I suppose, I must have lost seven or eight rabbits on that particular drop.

On that night we took home no rabbits at all, though I would not like it to be thought that it was usual for us to take home a fair bag. We had our good nights and our bad nights. I remember one particular night when it was foggy and I was sent to quarter the territory. I became utterly lost and confused. So much so that I began to "recognise" unfamiliar trees and I was eventually obliged to whistle for help from my companion who was a mite displeased. That venture also resulted in a blank return.

Long-nets, of course, are known to be the night operator's tool and it is true that they can be deadly at the right time in the right place, but a long-net can also be used during the daytime with ferrets or, on rare occasions, when rabbits are lying out a long way from home during the daylight. Rabbits can then be driven towards home and the set net.

When ferreting a long hedgerow with a large number of holes, it is very difficult to cover every hole with a purse-net. It means a lot of disturbance and a lot of discomfort, so probably the easiest way of doing it is to start at one end, after having set a long-net completely, straight through the hedge at the bottom end. The long-net should run, strictly-speaking, at right-angles to the hedgerow on both sides. Rabbits bolting and being disturbed nearly always make a run down the hedgerow and dive in to the warren at a later stage. If a rabbit continues to bolt, it usually races right down the hedgerow until the long-net, correctly set, entangles it. It's a good ploy and most times it works.

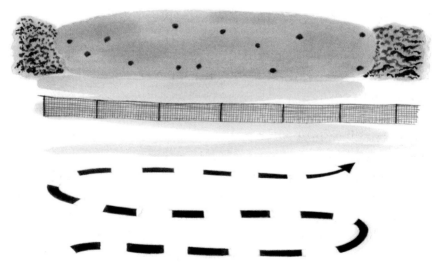

The long net is set about eight yards back from the warren when quartering a field after dark

On the odd occasion, however, there will be a rabbit or two which will bolt at right angles and make a run in the open field instead of continuing along the hedgerow. It is then advisable to run the long-net directly through the hedge at an angle. This may mean some cutting and clipping with secateurs but the net is then turned in the direction of the beginning of operations. It is set in a V-shape with the hedgerow running down the middle of it so any rabbits breaking to the right or left will be ensnared. It is not often necessary to do this but there are certain areas where the rabbits are inclined to break from cover and after a while one begins to recognise these situations.

I can remember once running a long-net through the hedgerow and turning it at, I suppose, about a 30 degrees angle on both sides up towards the operator. A 100-yard net allows 50 yards either side of the hedgerow which covers a lot of ground. It was one of those wild mornings when we more or less let caution go to the winds and took our chances. We whooped and hollered as rabbits bolted, and made them run very fast towards the set net. We caught 11 doing that and when the net was picked up and cleared, we used a line ferret and found another dead rabbit underground. That made a total of 12, of which 11 had bolted. That is when the long-net, in my opinion, is worth its weight in gold.

Where rabbits have to venture out, or are inclined to move out a long way, and sometimes pop through another hedgerow on their travels, it is very often possible to run a long-net across a big warren about 10 yards distant and then to go and walk the surrounding fields. It is amazing how a rabbit will sometimes lie out a long way from home. With a couple of terriers or a good dog quartering the ground, rabbits may be picked up or sent running towards the bury which is their home. The net will intercept them and it is well worth doing this on a day when the bury has to be ferreted later on so that the rabbits are sent underground. On the other hand, of course, why not catch them in the long-net first?

One of my most memorable long-netting outings, briefly mentioned in an earlier chapter, had nothing to do with the rabbits killed but the fact that it was carried out during the breeding season at entirely the wrong time. It had a purpose behind it, however. A local farmer had said to me that he had not a single rabbit on the farm and would I, therefore, try to put a few does down so that he could at least see a few bunnies hopping around.

Malcolm Baldwin and I went to a farm where we knew the rabbits were prone to lie out some distance and by running the long-net, with a hedgerow in between, we caught eight pregnant doe rabbits. This was one of my most enjoyable rabbit experiences but it was an awful job trying to catch a live rabbit, extract it from the long-net, put it into a sack and close the top while several other rabbits were struggling to escape in the long-net! However, I didn't lose one and we ended up with two sacks full of healthy, pregnant does, which we took down to the other farm at about 2 o'clock in the morning. We wandered over the fields to release them into an old, disused rabbit bury. In a few days time we saw several rabbits along that hedgerow, and it was not long before we were spotting young rabbits in numbers. For many years after that we had extremely good ferreting from the rabbits we had actually stocked ourselves.

The farmer who allowed us to use our long-net on that occasion had asked us particularly not to kill a ginger rabbit which lived in the territory we were to ransack. Of course, in the dark, we caught the ginger rabbit and I told the farmer that we had, in fact, taken it and released it on the other farm. He was quite happy about this. What was so annoying, however, was that the following year when we ferreted the territory, the first rabbit which our ferrets killed happened to be the big ginger doe!

Long-nets usually come in 100-yard lengths and there were men, I understand, who used two or as many as three. I think that these men were professionals whose livelihoods depended upon the rabbits they caught and sold. I have never been in that position, but I have carried a 100-yard net and backed it up with a 50-yarder as a matter of course, and for a little bit of insurance. The point I am trying to make, however, is that for each 100 yards length of long-net you will need an iron spike at each end of the net, and you will also need at least a dozen stakes, each about 2½ ft. long. Take my advice and learn to do everything in the daylight. Loop the net over the first iron peg so that it comes off when it is run out like cotton coming off a spool.

Always, when you drop a long-net, keep the top string tight because when you are running it off the spike you are ahead of the man who is responsible for putting in the stakes. If it is tight he will know which is the top string, and that is very important. My old tutor of many years ago always said to me "When you're dropping a string boy," (and of course by dropping a string he meant running a long-net) "always keep the top string tight, the bottom string will fall and make its own level. It will follow the contours of the ground below. Never, ever forget to keep the top string tight". I have remembered this advice and it has always worked for me.

Long-nets can be very useful pieces of equipment but they have to be worked with discretion. Do not, for instance, run one over a field that has been freshly combined. It will pick up every bit of loose straw and you will go home with a bundle of netting and tangled straw which takes a long time to sort out. After several uses the long-net must be pegged out in the daylight, and after rain, allowed to dry in the wind. There is more to looking after a long-net than sticking it in a sack and forgetting about it, for it can be an important piece of equipment. I would very hate much to be without mine.

RABBIT TOAD IN THE HOLE

I don't really like the name, but I can't think of a better one and you have my word for it that this is young rabbit at its best. Make this dish when you have to roast a big joint of prime beef and cook two meals in one. Lay a portioned rabbit in the bottom of the roasting dish, season lightly and put the beef joint directly on top of it. Roast and baste the joint in the normal way until it is tender, then remove it from the dish. The rabbit portions will meanwhile have absorbed much of the natural fat and juices from the beef and should be almost falling off the bones. Two choices are now open to you. You can serve the fresh roast beef or put it away for cold cuts later. Either way, leave the rabbit in with the beef juices. If you eat the beef there and then, set the rabbit portions, still in the roasting dish, aside for tomorrow. Re-heat it all in a hot oven and when thoroughly hot cover with a standard Yorkshire pudding batter mixture. Bake until the pudding has risen and is crisp. There will almost certainly be some sticking to the bottom of the roasting dish where the juices of the beef and rabbit have mingled, but that, if anything, enhances the meal.

CHAPTER 16

What, I wonder, constitutes a memorable rabbiting day? I remember many remarkable days ferreting but not all of them were concerned with counting the slain at the end of each one. When I have to judge a day's sport by the size of the bag, it will be time for me to quit.

One memorable day was the first time I used what was then known as a "bleeper" and lost two ferrets for the first and only time in over sixty years! I am not referring to the modern electronic equipment in use today but to those early, converted transistorised radios which supposedly let an operator know where his ferret was working. Waist-deep in nettles, and in a situation which I should not have tackled anyway, I followed the maniacal tack-a-tack-a-tack signals as well as I could and finally realised I had been sold a pup! Twenty-five miles away, as I sat down to my Sunday lunch, the lunatic unit was still tacking away, like an overheated nuclear reactor! I temporarily lost my faith in electronics and went back to using a traditional line-ferret in the old-fashioned style. A lot more work was involved but it was a great deal more reliable!

Ferreting, where there are large numbers of holes, involves a considerable amount of netting in advance and there are times when that kind of disturbance deters rabbits from bolting. This is particularly so at the tail-end of the season, when rabbits are pairing prior to breeding. It was in such circumstances that Malcolm Baldwin and I set a long-net through a well-occupied hedgerow to intercept rabbits bolting away and downhill to a corner sanctuary. For once a well-conceived plan worked. The rabbits bolted the way we wanted them to run, i.e. down and along the hedgerow itself. The long-net, set at right angles through a field gate, tripped up every escapee and we bagged a round dozen prime rabbits in the dead of winter. The work involved was next to nothing and the sporting side of the venture could not have been better planned. There is something very special about fleeing rabbits hitting a long-net in broad daylight and I regard that occasion as one of the highlights of my rabbiting life.

The following year, in exactly the same place, one rabbit bolted and was caught, and 11 more were located underground by traditional use of the line ferret. Again the bag was exactly a dozen. A long way down on the totem pole in terms of quarry in the bag but memorable because, with only one bolted rabbit, what looked like being a disastrous day was suddenly transformed into one of sporting success.

There are times when it is more or less essential to prove, by showing a heap of quarry, that ferreting is as good a way as any of controlling rabbits. The operative word is control and not extermination. I know many farmers who want to see rabbits controlled without extermination, and there are times when I have had to prove a point. It is of little use promising to reduce the rabbit population if it is not seen to have been reduced, and while this applies to farming in Britain, in Australia it is a different matter.

It is thought, by those who do not know the territory, that the whole of Australia is a moving mass of rabbits but this is true of only a few remote parts. In the main, the kangaroo does more damage in a night than a thousand rabbits do in a week, but we who know and love Australia have to accept that "the greenies", who think they know best, haven't a clue! All of which leaves a rabbit problem familiar to worried farmers but recognised as a sporting opportunity by ferreting men.

If I were so minded I could tell of an Aussie day of rabbit slaughter but instead I will settle for a day and a night that provided sport and pleasure for all concerned, as well as food in quantity for several months to come. It is not always easy to keep rabbit corpses fresh and free from flies in the outback areas of Western Australia but it is a matter of honour, among a hunters of like mind, that flesh is not allowed to deteriorate. All of which calls for careful planning in advance.

Ernie, Peter and I made camp just as the evening sun lost its real power. In the back of the utility truck, five ferrets nestled under their towelling blankets and enjoyed the cool air given off by the cola bottle which had been filled with water, frozen solid and left in their wire cage. Ernie and Peter left me to prepare the wind break, light the camp fire and bake the damper of flour, baking powder, salt and water, and also to be ready to deal with a rabbit supper when they returned. They were not long in doing so, and with three rabbits very quickly dressed out and put on ice, I lit the lantern and prepared supper as they went out again. Bacon, onion, tomato and rabbit portions, iced, floured and seasoned, were tossed in the Dutch camp oven before I put the lid on and covered it with hot coals. The damper baked steadily in the other oven and I poured myself a glass of Aussie red wine which, in the opinion of many friends, leaves French plonk for dead!

They came back at about 11.00pm with 18 rabbits which they had shot in the "spottie". I'd heard them in the distance and I knew they had ventured far, but I was not concerned. Ernie is a true bushie. He simply could not get lost, even if he tried.

If you've never sat round a camp-fire in the warmth of an Australian night and broken great chunks of damper to chew with succulent roast rabbit, you have not lived! It is an experience to be remembered and if it is enhanced with thoughts of an early morning ferreting session among the rabbits, it's one you will never forget!

It was still dark when we kicked the camp-fire into life, boiled a billy of black tea, gave the ferrets a drink of milk, and headed for the warrens in the distance. We had no nets, no lines and no bleepers. We were dressed in shorts, sneakers and T-shirts. The ferrets sensed the occasion and rabbits disappeared underground as we approached. With loaded shotguns and a very well-rehearsed safety procedure, we hunted through the day. The amazing part about it all was that the rabbits were in bolting mood at the outset and remained so all through the ensuing hours. I shot my share it is true but I had positioned myself so that the better shots could score. I spent most of my time picking up ferrets, gutting rabbits and putting them in wet sacks to keep off the flies. By mid-afternoon, the ferrets were tired, we operators were thirsty and the farmer, who had joined us briefly, was impatient. He had gathered several buckets of crayfish from his dams, the wine was on ice, the copper was boiling, and his wife was waiting to serve crayfish and salad.

We had taken 78 rabbits which, along with those shot the night before, made a total of 99. Could we not make it up to the round 100?

Not, apparently, without offending the farmer and his wife. Enough was enough it seemed and, fair go, there was all next weekend and the rest of the year to score a ton! The ferrets had more or less decided that enough was enough anyway and with crayfish, barbecued steaks and mulberry pie on the menu, what difference could another rabbit make, apart from being just one more carcass to paunch and skin. That's the trouble with the big numbers game. When it's all over, the work begins!

I remember one more special day in Australia when I did play quite a big part in the numbers game. It was a lengthy journey that Laurie Hateley, Bert Geddes and I took to the south of West Australia in order to spend a weekend rabbiting on an exceptionally infested farm. Again we took no nets, apart from half-a-dozen which I secreted for my own personal and occasional use while I was working the ferrets on the bury. We relied instead on our 12-bore shotguns and a large supply of cartridges, plus four jill ferrets which were good workers and always successful in bolting rabbits from these big warrens. We had a four-wheel drive truck, plenty of wet sacks and ample ice in cooler boxes ready for the day ahead. We also took with us some fresh tomatoes and fruit but we were relying upon catching some rabbits to roast for the evening meal. We intended, of course, to stay overnight and make a two-day excursion of it. We kept the ferrets in cages rather than in boxes and covered them with wet sacks so that they remained cool in the harsh environment.

It was a long way to the first bury, but it was a huge one and needed a deal of concentration on all our parts. We tipped in three ferrets and let them wander willy-nilly through the whole complex. The result was stunning! Rabbits bolted as I had never seen them bolt before. They did not hop from hole to hole but simply fled across the parched territory, one after the other. Laurie and Bert, being exceptionally good shots, killed 99 per cent of them as they ran. I took my share but I was more interested in working the ferrets, picking them up and putting them down different holes and making sure that they were not suffering. A springer spaniel and a labrador retrieved all the rabbits that were shot and gradually the pile increased by the end of the day. I covered them all after we had tied them down on the 'roo bars of the four-wheel drive and, by driving it around, cooled the carcasses and then put them in the wet sacks.

On one occasion during that day a springer spaniel played particular attention to one hole, much to the annoyance of its master, but I recalled occasions when it paid to watch the dog in the ferreting field. On this occasion I just slipped a net over the hole which he was watching and, sure enough, a rabbit bolted and I caught it. I snipped its ears with a pen-knife so that I knew which one had not been shot. This was a crafty move taught me by my old tutor many years ago. I made sure I had that one for supper!

It was a long and tiring day. Those two rabbit sportsmen, Bert and Laurie, followed it up with the spotlight to make the numbers up to the 200 which they had envisaged at the outset. Meanwhile I baked a damper and cooked some rabbits and chops for our evening meal. Again they were away a long time but I was not worried. They both knew their way around and the four-wheel drive was very reliable. We retired for the night after drinking a couple of bottles of really good Australian wine and sleeping under the stars. There was no danger of it raining. It was warm enough so we only needed one blanket apiece and our nights were spent very peacefully under the eucalyptus trees. We had a few more hours of busy activity during the next day and then decided to call it quits at around mid-day with a long journey home ahead of us

I recall taking 42 rabbits home to my daughter in Western Australia and arriving back at about 6 o'clock in the evening. I was absolutely exhausted but there was only one thing to do and that was to dress out those rabbits and put them on ice overnight so that the flesh did not in any way deteriorate. We formed a production line my wife, my daughter, my grand-daughter and me - after my son-in-law said "Bloody Hell!" and then promptly disappeared, knowing that there was some work ahead. I skinned the rabbits (they had already been gutted, of course) and we removed unwanted parts, while one of us went to the bottle house to return with two huge bags of ice. We then processed the rabbits in what was known as the Laundry Room where there were a couple of huge deep sinks and plenty of room to move. It worked out perfectly but I was tired out at the end of it. In fact we were all tired. However, we put the rabbit joints in the sinks, poured cold water on them and then tipped in the two bags of ice. There they stayed until they were put into the deep freeze the next day.

That is one of my most memorable occasions of rabbiting in the heat of Western Australia and the sandy soil. It was entirely different from the situation as it is in England and while don't suppose I will ever have another day like it, I live in hope!

89

COLD RABBIT PIE

Cold pies are excellent if made from half rabbit and half pork or ham. This is how I make mine. Trim the meat from the rabbit and cut into small cubes. Pressure-cook the remaining carcass to make a concentrated stock. Mix the rabbit meat with an equal amount of not-too-lean pork or ham. To each 1lb of meat add ¼lb of wholemeal bread (soaked and squeezed). Season liberally with salt, pepper and sage, then pack everything into a pie-crust made from hot-water pastry and moulded round an upturned jar. Cover and seal with a pastry lid. Bake for 15 minutes in a 450°F oven. Glaze with egg and lower the temperature to 325°F. Cook for a further 1½-2 hours, depending upon the size of the pie. Add 1 oz of gelatine or a pint of the concentrated stock and pour through the steam vent in the pastry lid. Allow to cool and set before cutting.

Ordinary short-crust pastry may be used instead of the hot-water pastry if the pie is made in a round cake-tin.

CHAPTER 17

I often wonder why many otherwise keen rabbiters do not opt to stay out all night or make a week-end camping trip out of their efforts with snares, traps or ferrets. Our winters are nowhere nearly as cold as they used to be and sleeping out over a winter period can be perfectly acceptable. Staying over on the job means that much more time can be spent working the territory involved.

I am, I confess, thinking back to the days when we did not jump into a warmed-up car to travel long distances to our rabbiting. We used to have to cycle, and 10 or 15 miles of pedal-pushing plus the weight of rabbits on our return was not something to which we looked forward, so we tended, in those days, to spend more time on the territory and less time travelling. I don't think it was a bad idea. It did not harm us in any way and I can remember crawling into a dry ditch, partly sheltered by briars and blackthorn and praying for the dawn to come. But I also remember nestling between two hay bales in a luxurious hayloft and praying for the dawn not to come, such was the comfort of my bedroom. I could actually feel the warmth creeping back into my bones after a hard day's sport with the ferrets in bitter cold. Haylofts were delightful places in which to bed down.

I suppose it depended on where you were and what you were actually doing which made the difference between wanting to go home or to stay. I remember once sitting in an open-fronted cow byre with two warm hay beds behind me. But instead of sleeping I stayed up all night with a companion around a small fire warming up soup, eating sandwiches and toasting bread. I simply did not want to retire. It was an adventure and has always seemed that way to me, and there is no reason why rabbiters shouldn't indulge in a similar fashion today.

Some time ago a friend and I, having been given special permission, pitched a couple of small bivouacs in the sheltered corner of our chosen rabbiting territory. We started by putting down a number of wires in a likely area then, on the Friday night, we ran the long-net, though with very poor results. We caught only a couple of rabbits, which hardly made it worth the effort, but the next day we prepared our traps and put them down in the early hours of the morning in one particular well-used warren, and hoped for the best. Then we took our two ferrets and proceeded to work some smaller buries along the hedgerows, while the traps and snares played their waiting game. Our ferreting procedure was very much the same as it had always been. We entered a loose jill, let her have a run around and bolt rabbits into the purse-nets. We then followed her up with a collared hob to dig out those that had been reluctant to bolt or had been killed on the spot.

However, our traps and snares remained empty, so we took the .22 rifle with the silencer and sub-sonic bullets and crept around various parts where we knew rabbits would be sitting out. This shooting foray was reasonably successful for we took half-a-dozen rabbits on the first evening. Then, as night fell, we went back to our tents and waited until the darkness had really fallen. It was approaching midnight before we moved again to inspect the traps and wires. This time we picked up two rabbits in the humane traps and several in the snares.

It was no big deal. We had many times caught more rabbits but it was rather nice to see 11 freshly-paunched and hocked rabbits hanging on the barbed-wire fence in the light of the old pressure lamp which we used to illuminate our camp-site. Strangely enough, despite the coldness of the weather, I was interested to note that several moths and many different flies were attracted towards the light of the lamp.

We were involved in only one complicated dig with the collared hob, which revealed two fairly mangled corpses where he had stayed with his quarry Meanwhile our traps and snares produced another half-a-dozen rabbits, two in particular from likely-looking runs in a fence.

It was like being a schoolboy again. Two old chaps, out and about in the morning, in the afternoon and in the dark hours doing what we loved and enjoying every moment of it, just like two boys let loose during the school holidays! It was a marvellous experience.

On the way home, in the warmth of the car, we discussed our bag. Nothing very special at all about this in view of the fact that it had taken us almost three days and the use of the ferrets, long-net, traps and wires to produce 19 rabbits, but it was genuine sport and we had worked for our reward.

As I have mentioned several times before, camping out and staying overnight or for two or three nights is par for the course during a rabbiting session in Australia. It means that we are with our equipment, our ferrets, our wires or whatever, and it also means that we are able to use what we catch and prepare meals for the camp without having to resort too much to bought-in produce. We refer to a rabbit cooked during one of these sessions as an "outdoor rabbit meal", but remember that the same principle can be applied to rabbits caught during a camping session in this country. In Australia it is a simple matter to skin a warm rabbit and cook it straight away. In England I think it is better to let it hang and cool down before cooking but, either way, if time is allowed for a casserole rather than a roast rabbit, it is perfectly adequate and may be used at anytime.

Let us assume that you have a rabbit for cooking outside. This is how I would prepare the meal, and how I have done it many times in Britain, America, Australia and Canada.

Cut up a rabbit and lay the portions on a square of kitchen foil. (Cut off any jagged or protruding bones to prevent the foil from puncturing.) Add a chopped onion and about ½ lb of streaky pork, or a few dabs of lard. Sprinkle with salt, black pepper and mixed herbs. Wrap it all up into a tight package. Now wrap up that package in another one, and toss it into the fire after the flames have died down a little and the embers are red. Keep the fire going by adding a little fuel now and then. Leave it for at least 20 minutes before turning it over. The moisture inside will prevent burning and the steam generated will cook the meat to tender perfection.

This is the real joy of such cooking. Shake off the ash from the outer layer of foil and unwrap it carefully. The inner wrapper should now be perfectly clean and free from ash or grit. Open it up, use it as a plate, eat the contents with your fingers and forget the washing up!

Barbecue units with meat cooking on the top grid can, of course, also be used for foil-wrapped cooking. Corn cobs, potatoes, onions and so on can be cooked in the coals while the meats are being prepared. The American outdoor cooking unit exposes the meat to the glowing coals and, with starter fuel and charcoal bricks as part of the deal, it is, to some extent, an artificial set-up. The Australian unit, however, which can be brick-built or made from a half-section of an oil drum, comprises a ¼ in thick mild steel hot plate beneath which a roaring log fire is built up. The plate heats up, burning off all the grease left from any previous meal and then, when it has cooled sufficiently, it is smeared with a little oil or fat and the meats are laid on top. Alongside the meats go onions, sliced tomatoes, cut bread rolls, sausages and underneath, in the embers, go the foil-wrapped jacket potatoes.

Rabbit so cooked in Australia would not be considered edible without the essential litre of ice-cold beer to help it down, and the correct and only way to tell if the hot plate is at the right temperature for cooking is to pour a spot or two of beer on it. If it disappears in a cloud of steam it's too hot, but if it stays long enough to begin to run, the temperature is just right.

I have cooked rabbit in every way imaginable in the Canadian wilderness, usually using a Dutch oven. I have worked with an ice-cold back and an oven-warmed front to produce rabbit pies, casserole and pasties. Each has been accompanied by damper bread made of flour, baking powder, salt and water, baked to perfection in the Dutch oven.

All food cooked thus has been appreciated by those present and I have no hesitation in saying that what applies to the rest of the world applies to the UK also. All it needs is the accompanying spirit of adventure!

RABBIT CROQUETTES

Mince the meat from a big tender rabbit and add an equal amount of minced beef. Add a cupful of plain boiled rice, bind with a beaten egg and season to taste. Mould into croquette shapes and fry or bake in a hot oven. If the mixture is too soft, add a little commercial packet stuffing and leave for a few minutes before shaping. The rusk content of the stuffing mix will absorb the excess moisture.

CHAPTER 18

The days are long gone when rabbits used to venture into the standing corn, remain there throughout the summer, have their young in the corn, feed on the green undergrowth and enjoy a perfectly safe environment. Their only predator was, of course, the fox. Charley would amble his way through the corn occasionally to come upon a litter of young, but for the most part rabbits, in quite large numbers, lived and bred during the summer months in the corn crop.

The harvest, when it came, was a notable day in the shooting man's calendar. He would make arrangements with the farmer to be present when the last of the corn was cut and the rabbits, which had been constantly driven into the centre of the field by the harvester, were obliged to make a bolt for it as the final strips of corn were cut when they were shot by standing Guns strategically placed. They were also bowled over by local villagers throwing sticks, and believe it or not, were sometimes chased on foot and caught by hand by people wearing running shoes or plimsolls. The reason they were able to achieve this feat was, of course, that the stubble was left about 6in high in those days and rabbits found it difficult to run over the stems. A man in plimsolls could run equally fast and if he was agile (and there were some nippy men about) he would catch a rabbit in his bare hands and kill it. It was a really exciting time, but there were also other ways of catching the rabbits during the harvesting season. Rabbits had vacated their buries around the surrounding fields to take up their residence in the corn but when they were assaulted at the end of the harvest the survivors made, once more, for their home territory. This was when we who sought rabbits were crafty enough to make provision for their capture!

Those summer-neglected holes were visited a few days before the final ejection of the rabbits from the corn and a number were completely blocked up, while others were made inaccessible, at arm's length, with pieces of old sacking, turves, or bundles of hay. This meant that a running rabbit, escaping the Guns, sticks or runners, would seek refuge and run for cover into one of these open holes, not knowing that it was blocked about a yard inside.

This ploy was so successful that, in fact, we who hunted rabbits by all manner of means occasionally took as many as three rabbits from each hole. Several times we caught as many as eight or nine rabbits after the end of the harvest shoot, simply by visiting the blocked-up buries. Sometimes we would wait until after dark before we went to work, for occasionally harvest rabbits took cover in hedgerows elsewhere and did not dive underground until the Guns and farm labourers had departed. We marked the blocked-in buries with white sticks or stones and then, just before it became really dark, we checked these areas. It was quite an adventure. In fact, it was really more exciting doing it in the dark than during the daytime. Either way it didn't really matter because these were prime rabbits, collected and harvested.

Another way of taking rabbits could be effective pretty well all the year round. Where any deep, dry ditch crossed a field gate it would be piped, and rabbits often used to take up residence in this pipeline. It was a sanctuary for them and they stayed there. By peeping through you could sometimes see a pair of ears and so be sure that there was a rabbit present. We then cut a long length of stiff, fence wire, poked it through the drainpipe and left it there. The wire weathered and rusted until the rabbits got used to it being there and took no notice of it. Then, at a later date, on our walk round, we would look along the tunnel and, if we saw a rabbit was present we would bend a section of stiff, bramble or hawthorn so that it would absolutely cram its way through the pipe on one end of the wire. We would then pull on the other end of the wire, dragging the piece of bush with it and, of course, the rabbit was bound to be pulled through. We had to be very careful and swift to catch the live rabbit before it escaped. At times we were lucky and there might be as many as two rabbits in a pipe. It was a simple, wily wheeze which worked very well over a number of years and still, to this day, works in certain places. Sometimes you can out-smart a rabbit. It doesn't happen very often though, but it is well worth recording when it does!

"A simple wily wheeze!"

Throughout my long life rabbits have, for me, been a source of sport, of good food and the means of creating great friendships in this country and in far-off Australia, and I raise my hat to this sometimes under-estimated, but essential part of our countryside. Long may rabbits thrive and long may they provide sport, excitement and fine fare.

ROAST RABBIT

Fill the belly cavity of a young, tender rabbit with your favourite stuffing, or with sausage meat, season well, cover with strips of belly-pork or streaky bacon and cook in a hot oven. When the pork has crisped, remove it and allow the rabbit to brown, basting periodically with the juices in the roasting dish. Quite delicious!